BLOGGING AMERICA

POLITICAL DISCOURSE IN A DIGITAL NATION

Barbara O'Brien

WILLIAM, JAMES & CO.

Dedication

To Sean and Erin.
—B.O'B.

Publishers	Bill Hoffman (william_hoffman@wmjasco.com)
	Jim Leisy (james_leisy@wmjasco.com)
Production	Tom Sumner
Marketing	Christine Collier
Order Processing	Krista Brown

Printed in the U.S.A.

William, James & Co. is an imprint of Franklin, Beedle & Associates, Inc.

Library of Congress Cataloging-in-Publication
data available from the publisher.

ISBN (softcover) 1-59028-040-7
ISBN (softcover) 1-59028-042-3

C O N T E N T S

Chapter 4   139
Best of the Blogs
Part 1: Blogging the Economy

Part 2: Divided We Blog   156

Appendix: The Clark Sphere   195
Epilog: The Way of Blogs   200
Glossary of Blogging Terms   203

P R E F A C E

———◆——◆——◆——◆——◆———

THIS BOOK CELEBRATES political blogging in America. It approaches blogging as a multi-faceted phenomenon that encompasses journalism and media, political discourse and commentary, rhetoric and debate.

What Is a Blog?

A *blog*, short for *web log*, is a personal journal made publicly available on the web. Bloggers write about their own lives, their families, their pets, and their hobbies.

And bloggers express *opinions*—about politics, candidates, current events, the economy, social issues, and everything else in the news. And the words bloggers write are available to readers around the globe. Before you dismiss blogging as little more than an outlet for creative self-expression, consider this—just six of the most popular political blogs (A Political Animal, Daily Kos, Eschaton, Instapundit, and Talking Points Memo) are visited by more than a half million people every day.

Yes, that's six bloggers, more than five hundred thousand readers. *Daily.* Some bloggers have a bigger readership than many major newspaper columnists. And readership of blogs will likely increase as more people gain access to high-speed Internet.

The opinions expressed by popular bloggers spread quickly to other blogs. For example, a comment by Glenn Reynolds of Instapundit may be quoted on a hundred other conservative blogs, and discussed on Internet forums and in chat rooms, and thereby seen by countless more readers. And from there, one man's point of view fans out to water coolers, dinner tables, and barrooms across the nation.

We, the People, are talking back.

About This Book

Chapter 1 explains blogging and discusses how blogs are already impacting politics and journalism. Chapter 2 serves as a beginner's guide to the Blogosphere, mapping the way to a few popular sites of the Right and Left.

The remainder of the book is anthology. My goal is not only to present examples of blogs as literature, but also to demonstrate how bloggers shape opinion and facilitate discussion. The reader can compare the perspectives of several bloggers on the same news story, such as the 2004 State of the Union Address, or on issues such as the proposed "protection of marriage" amendment. The examples reveal both the quality of blogging and how real dialogue is emerging among bloggers and their readers.

I admit that publishing web literature on a paper-and-ink page is a little like writing on clay tablets about digital graphic reproduction. Links are an integral part of web documents, and removing the links diminishes them. Throughout I have inserted endnotes with URLs to the linked pages, in lieu of links. Clunky, I know, but for now it will have to do.

About the Links in This Book

There are many links to web pages in this book. Admittedly, most of them are too cumbersome to type out. To ease the strain, go to the web page www.wmjasco.com/bloglinks.html for a list of clickable links for web sites and web pages listed in the footnotes and endnotes of this book.

Acknowlegments

While combing through the Blogosphere looking for material for this book, I made every effort to represent many points of view, *especially* those different from mine. I have tried to treat all bloggers with equal respect, and to present each blog fairly so that readers may form their own conclusions about the opinions expressed.

But I am a blogger also, and a *known element* of the liberal half of the Blogosphere. I regret that a few bloggers of the right were reluctant to trust me and withheld permission to publish their work. For this reason I am especially grateful to the conservative bloggers who agreed to appear in this book. I sincerely hope they are pleased when they see their words in print. (And, of course, I am also grateful to the bloggers represented here with whom I *agree*.)

Thanks also to the people at William, James & Co.—Jim, Bill, Tom, Chris, Krista, Dean—who encouraged me to write this book

Finally, I want to thank, and apologize to, bloggers whose work I admire and read every day, but who are not represented elsewhere in this book. These include (but are not limited to): Steve M. of No More Mister Nice Blog (http://nomoremister.blogspot.com), who has a genius for turning news stories inside out to reveal their inner absurdities; Jeanne d'Arc of Body and Soul (http://bodyandsoul.typepad.com/blog), one of the most graceful writers on the web; Michael Miller of Public Domain Progress (www.publicdomainprogress.info), who prods me into being a less *wimpy* liberal; and whoever it is that writes Fafblog (http://fafblog.blogspot.com) for explaining the universe.

You make the world a better place.

PROLOG

Why Blogs?

———◆———◆———◆———

"The Revolution Will Be Blogged"

—*AndrewSullivan.com*

IN OCTOBER 2003, THE WHITE HOUSE launched the Great Media Blitz to tell the story of U.S. success in Iraq. If you don't remember the Great Media Blitz, don't worry. Your memory is fine. It was the blitz that fizzled.

The Bush Administration had become annoyed with news from Iraq provided by regular news media channels and decided to go around them. "I'm mindful of the filter through which some news travels," President Bush told an interviewer, "and sometimes you just have to go over the heads of the filter and speak directly to the people."[1]

But how did the White House go about speaking "directly to the people?" I noted on The Mahablog (www.mahablog.com) on October 13, 2003:

> Did you notice that none of the usual White House suspects showed up for yesterday's Sunday morning news programs? In recent weeks, Condi and Colin and even Dick have been "interviewed" nearly every Sunday by

---

[1] Richard Wolffe and Rod Nordland, "Bush's News War," *Newsweek*, October 19, 2003 (http://msnbc.msn.com/id/3225672).

> Tim and Wolf and George. And these "interviews" have been a great source of merriment, I must say.
>
> But now the White House is supposed to be engaged in a PR blitz to sell the Iraq War. Why did they bypass the Sunday morning news programs? Isn't that a little weird?
>
> Last week Dick preached to the choir at the Heritage Foundation and Condi spoke to the Chicago Council on Foreign Relations and Dubya his own self spoke to Air National Guard in New Hampshire. Some blitz.[2]

The White House embarked on a multi-pronged media offensive. First, President Bush and senior officials stopped giving interviews to the big national and international media establishments and instead called in local television reporters, who tend to be gentler questioners. Second, congressional allies and cabinet officials were dispatched to Baghdad so they could send home upbeat reports. And third, the President and his closest advisers fanned out around the country to speak to carefully vetted groups of ideological fellow travelers and adoring campaign contributors, presumably with favorable local news coverage in mind.

The result of the blitz was that, for most of us, the White House dropped out of the news entirely for a few days. I would never have known what they were up to if I hadn't been surfing the web to keep track of Bush Administration activities. And in spite of the blitz, news stories from Iraq did not become noticeably more positive. After a few days of blitzing, White House officials began to turn up on the Sunday morning talk shows again. The Great Media Blitz quietly was abandoned.

The blitz experiment reminds us that getting a message from a sender to a receiver requires a medium. And when a sender wants his message to reach millions of people, he needs a big, powerful medium. For the past few decades, those wishing to speak to the entire nation have relied on the mass media establishment—radio and television

---

[2] http://www.mahablog.com/2003.10.12_arch.html

networks, major newspapers, and wire services—to carry their messages.

In the Great Media Blitz example, the White House took action because the people were not receiving the message about Iraq the White House wanted them to receive. Whether this message failure was caused by media bias or incompetence, or whether the fault was with the message itself, is a matter for someone else's book. For now, let's consider the real purpose of the Great Media Blitz, which was not to "speak directly to the people" (presidents can get network air time to address the nation nearly any time they want it, except maybe during the Super Bowl) but to gain tighter control of the news "message" coming out of Iraq.

In an essay you can find in the appendix to this book, Stirling Newberry describes how the "television age" of the late 20th century created a top-down form of mass communication. And this, in turn, changed the political landscape of America.

> The power of media was that it could electrify the nation like a shock. For a nation that built its political and economic system on mobilizing people, the top-down media seemed like the answer—it could, for a short time, focus the entire attention of the nation on one problem, one social ill, and give it a face that could be remembered.
>
> This media gradually forced a few specific forms of campaigning; it also forced the drive for absolute and total control over every aspect of message—one loose image, and the ship of state sinks . . . I remember the day the infamous tank picture came out in the Dukakis campaign, someone remarked "Great, we are working for snoopy the wonder beagle." From the Next President of The United States, to a joke, in moments.[3]

Top-down communication flows one way—from the top, down. We, the People, became passive recipients of the messages. And as

---

[3] Stirling Newberry, "The Clark Sphere," http://theclarksphere.com/archives/000249.html.

control of the message tightened, political discourse changed from being a means of debate to being a tool for manipulation. Radio and television in particular have been taken over by the designated spokes-persons of powerful political factions, and their assignment is to inflame the audience against the opposing powerful political factions.

Political communication was once exemplified by the Lincoln-Douglas debates. Today it has dissolved into sound bytes and talking points and the same few partisan "pundits" yelling over each other.

Those at the top care only that we receive their message correctly so that we continue to support them. Polls and focus groups are less about finding out what We, the People, think, than about learning how to fine-tune messages so that We, the People, think as we are supposed to.

But while the powerful few have struggled to gain tighter control of mass media, a new medium for political dialogue has emerged—the Internet. This new medium cultures robust political dialogue among people across the nation and around the world. And leading this discussion—generating topics, presenting information, and facilitating new perspectives—are *bloggers*.

Political discussion on the Internet pre-dates the web. As soon as home computers came with modems, people with opinions got online and expressed them. But now we are on the threshold of something new—the web as a big, powerful, and easily accessible medium that is *outside* the top-down media establishment.

Politicians ignore it at their peril. And yet, some still ignore it.

Even some politicos who are supposed to be web savvy don't "get" the real power of the web. In January 2004 Max Fose, Internet adviser to Senator John McCain's 2000 presidential campaign, was asked by an interviewer what to expect on the web from the Bush campaign. "I think what you're going to see is the 800-pound gorilla come out of the closet once the Democratic nominee is chosen, and that 800-pound gorilla is going to be George Bush and his Internet campaign," he said.

> The Bush campaign has an email list that's the largest in politics. It's larger than MoveOn. It's larger than the Democratic National Committee's. It's larger than any of the Democratic candidate's. And they're going to

> use that to mobilize, to blog, to raise money, and ev-
> erything the Bush campaign needs to do. They're go-
> ing to use the Internet to make it happen more effec-
> tively and be able to track the results.[4]

Max Fose continued to rhapsodize about the advantages of email over direct mail, then continued,

> Once the nominee is chosen on the other side, you're
> going to see the switch turned on, and the switch is
> going to be fund raising, and the means of activism—
> letters to the editor, calls to talk radio—and it's going
> to be a message sent out by the Bush campaign that
> isn't going to be filtered through the media. It's going
> directly to the inboxes of 6 million people.[5]

To be fair, Fose mentioned campaign blogs during the interview. But it was clear that, to him, an Internet campaign meant email linked to the candidates' web site, where email recipients could read the campaign's message and donate money. The message of the campaign goes one way—from the campaign managers to the supporters. Supporters are then expected to be walking billboards for the campaign message as well as ATM machines.

The official Bush-Cheney re-election campaign site (www.georgewbush.com) has a "blog" that reads like a string of press releases—the most recent post as I write begins, "The President and Mrs. Bush host a State dinner for the Nation's Governors at the White House." But a real blog is a *personal voice*—one writer expressing his thoughts to the world in his own unique style. I question whether announcements of state dinners written in a homogenous manner by a staff of writers is a blog at all.

Further, as of this writing the Bush-Cheney blog does not allow for public comments, which is a common feature of real blogs. Communication still flows only one way, from the campaign to the supporters. In

---

[4] Interview by Christopher Lydon, "The Blogging of the President," Minnesota Public Radio, January 25, 2004 (www.mpr.org/bloggingthepresident).

[5] *Ibid.*

contrast, the election site blog of the Democratic nominee-presumptive Senator John Kerry (http://www.johnkerry.com) is commented upon quite robustly. The blog itself still seems a bit contrived, however.

On the other hand, the recent campaign by Governor Howard Dean made creative and extensive use of web resources, including blogs. Dean supporters were *not* passive recipients of Dean's message. Through the web, supporters played a tactical role in the campaign. Dean campaign managers learned that attempting centralized management of the web campaign created bottlenecks that slowed growth, so they stopped trying to micromanage the network and got out of its way. The result was a "smart mob" of dedicated supporters who organized themselves and gave the Dean campaign momentum.[6]

But did the smart mob contribute to the Dean campaign's eventual failure? Although a large turnout of Dean supporters showed up for the caucuses in Iowa, they failed to persuade non-wired Iowa voters to caucus for Dean. Postmortems of the Dean campaign are ongoing, but it is widely believed in the Blogosphere that Dean supporters were a little too self-directed and failed to stay on message. Others speculate that "Deaniacs" became so wrapped up in communicating with each other on the web that they forgot to reach out to the rest of the nation. And perhaps the fault was not mainly with the web, but with the candidate, or some other part of the campaign. Still, expect to see the Dean campaign's innovations studied and used in future campaigns.

It may be that in 2004 the Bush Administration, which by some accounts is so "on message" even cabinet meetings are scripted, will prevail in the election. However, I believe that by 2008 the web will have such an impact that a top-down, message-controlled presidential campaign will no longer be possible. Campaigns and their messages will originate not just with the parties, but also with the people. And by giving people a new way to engage in politics, the web could bring about a revitalization of democracy in America.

---

[6] See Gary Wolf, "How the Internet Invented Howard Dean," *Wired*, January 2004.

C H A P T E R 1

Storming the Bastille?

◆━━━◆━━━◆━━━◆━━━◆

A RECURRING SCENE in the film *Jefferson in Paris* shows aristocrats chatting about politics, oblivious to the peasants fomenting revolution in the streets. A similar scene is playing out today. Heads of political parties and owners/managers of traditional news media have yet to acknowledge there's a rebellion Out There. The Internet, after all, has been around for several years, and political weblogs (more commonly called *blogs*) date from the late 1990s. No heads have rolled—yet.

Well, maybe one head. It was the work of bloggers that brought about the 2002 resignation of Trent Lott as Senate Majority Leader. Senator Lott had made incendiary comments during a 100th birthday party for Senate colleague Strom Thurmond—comments that passed unnoticed by the Washington press corps. But not unnoticed by bloggers.

Senator Lott's remarks seemed innocent on the surface. "I want to say this about my state. When Strom Thurmond ran for president, we voted for him. We're proud of it. And if the rest of the country had followed our lead, we wouldn't have had all these problems over all these years, either."

Bloggers, notably Joshua Micah Marshall of Talking Points Memo (www.talkingpointsmemo.com) and Atrios[1] of Eschaton (www.atrios. blogspot.com), picked up this quotation and provided context— specifically, that Strom Thurmond had run for president in 1948 on a segregationist platform. In one campaign pamphlet unearthed by Atrios, Senator Thurmond had warned that the election of Harry Truman would mean "anti-lynching and anti-segregation proposals will become the law of the land and our way of life in the South will be gone forever." Senator Lott had, in effect, endorsed racial segregation and worse.

The story spread throughout the web like a firestorm. Five days later it was finally picked up by *The New York Times*. The rest truly is history.

Oliver Burkeman wrote in *The Guardian*, "The controversy has proved a defining moment for the vibrant online culture of weblogs— nimble, constantly updated, opinion-driven Internet journals, freed from many of the constraints of the established media."[2]

The Trent Lott story illustrates one thing political bloggers often are doing better than traditional, "professional" media—providing context. Another example: After the August 14, 2003, power blackout in which 50 million people lost electricity, print and broadcast media reported that the failure originated at First Energy Corporation of Ohio. But my own Mahablog (www.mahablog.com) scooped the world with details on the political ties between First Energy executives and the George W. Bush Administration.

Bloggers also keep stories alive after they have dropped off major media radar. For example, as I write, several bloggers are keeping tabs on the investigation of who leaked the identity of CIA undercover agent Valerie Plame. Plame's husband, Joseph Wilson, became a political enemy of the George W. Bush administration when he published a commentary in *The New York Times* revealing his investigation of the alleged sale of unprocessed uranium from Africa to Iraq. Wilson reported to the Bush Administration that the allegation was false, yet this claim later turned up in the President's 2003 State of the Union Address as a justification for invading Iraq to overthrow Saddam Hussein. The outing of Plame was a big news story in September, but for months it has disappeared from television and radio news and newspapers without resolution.[3]

Some stories are followed by bloggers long before they receive attention in major media. A number of bloggers labored for months to bring to light source code and other problems with electronic "black box" voting machines, currently being used in elections around the country. Only recently has a small part of this information broken through to newspapers.

Birth of Blogs

Blogs were born sometime after the World Wide Web came online in 1991. Rebecca Blood in *The Weblog Handbook*[4] identifies Mosaic's What's New page (online 1993–1996) as the progenitor of the format, although blogs weren't recognized as a distinct type of web site until 1998.

Through most of the 1990s blogging required skill with writing code, and most early blogs focused on technology. But by the late 1990s easy-to-use software—for example, the web-based tool Blogger, which launched in 1999—made blogging possible for the technologically challenged. Creating a web page became no more difficult than keyboarding.

Widespread use of Blogger and other blogwriting tools led to standardized formatting conventions. New entries are at the top of the web page. Older stuff sinks to the bottom and eventually scrolls off into archives organized by date. At this writing, state-of-the-art blogging comes with date stamps and permalinks (permanent links; that is, hyperlinks that point to a specific entry, not the page or site in general). Readers may leave public comments. Through RSS (Rich Site Summary) feeds, readers can subscribe to favorite blogs and have new entries delivered by email or to their desktops. And there are individual blogs, group blogs, blog alliances, and blogs that link and dialogue with other blogs. A vast network of news and commentary is growing out of sight of the traditional media.

There is no standardization of content. People blog about themselves, their professions, their hobbies, their families. There are blogs dedicated to issues and causes. And there are blogs that focus on politics.

What blogs can do:

- ► Blogs respond more quickly to breaking news than print media and usually provide commentary faster than radio or television.
- ► Bloggers collect and combine information and perspectives from many sources, including other blogs, resulting in a "meta-view" of current events.
- ► Bloggers act as news editors for their readers by linking to relevant news items and screening out the rest.

► Blogs are interactive and interconnected. Blogs are a medium for dialogue between bloggers and readers, and readers with other readers, and bloggers with other bloggers and *their* readers.

► Blogs restore a degree of individuality lost in corporate-owned media.

► Blogs are proving to be a useful tool for political campaigns and issue advocacy.

The down side—because there are no editors, the quality of writing and fact checking can be, shall we say, uneven (although one can say the same thing about traditional media). Some bloggers generate original content, but others provide little more than links and articles pasted from elsewhere. Copyright infringement is rampant. And because readers flock to blogs that best express their own opinions, the blosophere has become sharply divided between Left and Right—mirroring the political divisions of the non-virtual world.

A Word About Links

More than anything else, links distinguish writing for the web from writing on paper. Linking technology is more than just a handy-dandy referencing tool. Links are not just a feature of the web; they *are* the web. Blogs live and die by their links.

Nearly all blogs feature a blogroll of links to other blogs favored by the blogger. And because blogs with related content link to each other, readers can browse through several blogs as easily as browsing a single web site, or flipping the pages of a magazine. In effect, blogs linked together form an ad hoc online magazine with perpetually changing content.

Linking impacts writing in countless subtle ways. Bloggers not only distill information; they link to the sources of their information. The reader easily can click to the source and judge its quality. If a blogger criticizes a news story the reader can click to the original story and read it for himself. This fact makes blogging uniquely transparent and challenges bloggers to be honest.

This is especially true for blogs that allow readers to leave comments. A reader who catches an error on a blog will publicly point it out in a comments section attached to the blog article. Compare that to newspapers, in which an error and the correction are separated by time and space into different editions. Since bloggers often monitor each other, a blog-generated story that is inaccurate is quickly slapped down by other blogs.

"You've got transparency at all levels," said blogger Glenn Reynolds (Instapundit, www.instapundit.com). "And the beauty of the link is that if people don't agree with you, or wonder whether they should trust you, they can follow the link and read it for themselves and make up their minds. And that's true for most of what's on blogs. … It is a much more open and transparent field than any kind of journalism that we've ever had before."[5]

Which leads us to …

Blogs Versus Journalism

> The reporters I've talked to deride blogs as bloviating nonsense, worthless analysis, Ohio residents in their underwear with strong opinions.
> —Matt Stoller, The Blogging of the President
> (www.bopnews.com)

On the evening of January 19, 2004, I flipped on the television and settled down to watch news coverage of the Iowa Caucus. I watched the usual Talking Heads fill air time by discussing the Democratic presidential campaign as if it were a horse race — who's in the lead, who's expected to close the gap, who might fade in the stretch, and so on. After a while I went to my computer and soon found blogging from *within* caucuses. Caucus goers with laptops provided a moment-to-moment narrative as delegates were chosen. It was a *lot* more interesting. And on other blogs I found open debate on issues and the candidates' backgrounds.

Flip back to the television. The pundits were still talking about a horse race. No discussion of issues, little information on where the candidates stood on issues, no background information on the candidates. Just endless chatter about who's ahead and who's behind and what strategies the campaign managers would be using to keep their thoroughbreds—I mean, candidates—competitive.

Jay Rosen, professor of journalism at New York University, describes the patterns of what passes as campaign coverage in our time:

> The Gaffe: when a candidate on the campaign trail takes a pounding in the press for something that just isn't said to the press on the campaign trail.
>
> The Expectations Game: when a candidate "wins" by losing but doing better than the press expected, or "loses" by winning but doing worse.
>
> The Horse Race: when the press centers its coverage around shifts in who's ahead, based on poll results the press says are bound to shift.
>
> The Ad Watch: when the press converts political advertisements—and the strategy behind them—into political news, and then analyzes that news to advertise its own savviness.
>
> Inside Baseball: when the press tells the story of politics by going to insiders, the "players" who know the game because they play the game and get paid to know it.
>
> Electability News: when the press shifts from reporting on a candidate's bid for election in the here and now, to the chances of the bid succeeding later on.
>
> Spin Alley: when, after a debate, the press shows up in the spin room to be spun by stand-ins and spokespeople who are gathered there to spin the press.[6]

Here's a paragraph from a newspaper story that combines several of the above:

> With Dean faltering as the perceived front-runner, President Bush's campaign is thinking about how to run against the other Democratic contenders. If Dean rebounds, they'll cast him as an unstable liberal. If it's

Edwards, they'll highlight his inexperience with national
security issues. If it's Kerry, they'll paint him as a Massachusetts liberal. Said Grover Norquist, an anti-tax activist with close ties to the White House: "Kerry is a
taller version of (former presidential candidate and
Massachusetts Gov. Michael) Dukakis. He's a slimmer
version of Ted Kennedy."
> "Hot Off the Trail," Knight-Ridder, January 23, 2004

How about telling us something about what sort of men Dean,
Edwards, or Kerry actually are? How about providing information on
where they stand on issues? Is that too much to ask?

In 2000, we were subjected to catty remarks about Al Gore's earth
tone suits, or Al Gore misrepresenting the price of dog medicine, and
endless chatter about who was up or down in the polls and what
strategies the candidates would use. And hardly anyone—nobody on
television, for sure—actually did the work of investigating the candidates and their proposals.

It's not as if journalism were ever a pure and noble profession in
selfless service to the people. It's had its moments, of course, and there
have been many journalists through the years who have done excellent
work. But there have also been lazy and incompetent reporters and
media owners who imposed their biases on what was published or
broadcast. This isn't new.

And it's not hard to see the forces corrupting news media today.
Ownership of media is concentrated in fewer and fewer hands, eliminating competition. In television and radio, news departments have
been merged into entertainment divisions. The pundits covering
Washington politics move in the same social circles as the politicians
they cover. All of this has given us political reporting that is bland and
superficial at best and deliberately misleading at worst. And it is often
worst.

Still, when I consider the quality of journalism so far in the 2004
election cycle, I wonder—*do these people not realize what schlock this is?*
Those at the top of the profession, the famous faces who do the big

interviews and conduct the debates, do little more than try to trip candidates into misspeaking to get easy story hooks. Younger reporters can't seem to see past the spin *du jour* and who is up or down in the polls.

Kay McFadden of *The Seattle Times* wrote[7] about the dismal reporting of the Iowa caucuses. John Kerry's victory was not only an "occasion for trotting out comeback clichés. It also vindicated the media's obsession with electability as chief plank in the Democratic platform."

And this, writes McFadden, "gets television off the hook. It enables the blow-dried battalions to emphasize their greatest strength— handicapping—and veer away from complicated issues." And coverage of Howard Dean's unexpected third-place finish in Iowa "fulfilled TV's need to shape news events into high-pitched drama, while lessening the burden of dissecting a candidacy in terms more complex than 'anger issues.'"

I started blogging in 2002 out of sheer frustration with the quality of what passes for political journalism these days. I wanted a diversity of perspectives. I wanted political coverage with substance. There were hard questions I wanted asked that journalists were not asking. And I thought, if the mainstream press won't do it, I'll do it myself.

At this stage of blog evolution, blogs are not the same thing as journalism. As a rule (and this may change) bloggers do not do the information gathering and interviewing that reporters do. Rather, we supplement news media by providing context and analysis the "pros" miss.

> The weblog's strength is fundamentally tied to its position outside of mainstream media: observing, commenting, and honestly reacting to both current events and the media coverage they generate. Weblogs can function as superb digests of online material. They excel at exposing and explaining flaws in media coverage.
> —Rebecca Blood[8]

Further, I think the direct, raw, and unfiltered quality of blogging gives it energy and power missing from newspaper writing. Kevin Drum spoke to this in his blog Calpundit (Drum has since moved his blogging to A Political Animal, www.washingtonmonthly.com). He examined a newspaper account of something Wesley Clark said about rival John Kerry:

> One of the problems with print journalism is that there are certain stylistic constraints on how stories are written, and this one is a good example: in order to sound like professional writing, it weaves around the story in an oddly circuitous way, starting with a quote fragment, then an opinion, then a longer version of the quote, then an aside about Kerry's Vietnam service, then another piece of Clark's statement, and then finally a passing reference to the question that this was a response to.
>
> This is typical of news writing, in which it is somehow forbidden to just flatly get to the point and explain exactly what happened (a problem, by the way, that is especially acute in any story with numbers in it).[9]

I hope that blogging will become influential enough that the "professionals" have to compete with us. Then the blow-dried battalions will have to do some real political reporting.

Why America Needs Bloggers

Jay Rosen wrote in his blog Pressthink (http://journalism.nyu.edu/pubzone/weblogs/pressthink):

> Presidential campaigns had drifted out of alignment with most Americans. The ritual no longer seemed like something the country did for itself every four years, but what a professional cadre did, and sold back to the country as "politics."[10]

I can remember when the party national conventions actually chose the presidential nominee. No, really. Delegates came to the conventions pledged to a candidate but free to change their minds. Representatives of the contenders roared into the convention halls, and they wheeled and dealed and politicked, sometimes in back rooms and sometimes in front of cameras, until somebody got enough delegates to bag the nomination. It was a hoot to watch, I can tell you.

Then came reforms of the 1970s and 1980s, and today delegates come to the conventions locked into the candidate chosen by state primaries. The reforms were supposed to make the nominating process more "democratic." Instead, a small cadre of party insiders and their professional hired help learned how to manipulate the primary process to return a desired outcome.

Politics has become just another kind of marketing. And the party bosses—we don't call them bosses any more, of course, but that's what they are—choose the product, and marketing experts create the packaging and advertising to sell the product. Those at the top of the power pyramid use print and broadcast media, television in particular, to persuade a carefully focus-grouped public to support their candidate. Thus in the 2000 general election campaign, writes Rosen, "two almost identical campaigns, reading from the same data about the same issues, shouting at the same undecided voters in the same toss up-states, tried to ride slightly different catchwords into the White House."[11]

Political consultant Dick Morris calls this the "Media Age" style of campaign. "From 1972 to 1999 or 2000 we had what I see as the Media Age in American politics, which empowered guys like me who do television commercials, fundraisers, fat-cat donors, special interests and a handful of people who became the new political elite."[12]

Today, Morris continues, "the media is losing its power in politics, and the Internet is gaining it."

It's more accurate, I think, to say the web is creating a means for people to re-engage in the political process. To be sure, blogs have not dislodged the political elite. In the contest for the 2004 Democratic presidential nomination, the web advanced two candidates—Gov. Howard Dean and Gen. Wesley Clark—who seemed promising at first but who faded as actual primary votes were cast. Yet, although the web didn't produce a nominee, the Dean campaign in particular showed what was *possible*. Through the web, the Dean campaign raised

$45 million, which for a time caused the "old" media to sit up and take notice.

According to former Dean campaign manager Joe Trippi, broadcast politics fails the American people because it suppresses serious debate of issues in favor of politics as entertainment.

> It's a system that frankly back in the 1960s we had the Nixon-Kennedy debate and everybody should have understood then; it took about five to ten years to realize that was the moment when television was going to change everything in America's politics. What no one could've predicted was that it would have become a race for money, a race to buy a one-way communications tool that would take the American people essentially out of the process. It was no longer about average Americans, it was about, "How do I find a rich guy to write me a $2,000 check and then how do I take that money and buy television with it?" [13]

As I write, journalists and bloggers both are dissecting and analyzing the Dean campaign to determine how it failed, and also how it succeeded. Some argue that Governor Dean had flaws as a candidate that were unrelated to the web campaign. Others have pointed out that Dean's mostly young and technologically savvy volunteers did not connect well with the voters of Iowa and Vermont.

Still, as Scott Rosenberg wrote in *Salon*:

> Dean's campaign cannot be simply written off as a burst dot-com bubble. However few delegates the candidate ultimately wins, he long ago changed history. He taught his fellow Democrats, in Trippi's words, "how to be an opposition party"—and he forced his party to face the gulf between its leaders in Congress, who'd mostly supported Bush's Iraq war, and its voters, who largely didn't. He filled that "vacuum of debate" with a clamor that could not be ignored. [14]

Influencing the Influencers

The Institute for Politics, Democracy & the Internet of the Graduate School of Political Management at The George Washington University released a study of Internet citizenship in February 2004. Online Political Citizens (OPCs) are "Internet-oriented and politically energized" people who read blogs and participate in Internet discussion groups. OPCs, the study found,

> ... are nearly seven times more likely than average citizens to serve as opinion leaders among their friends, relatives, and colleagues. OPCs are disproportionately "Influentials," the Americans who "tell their neighbors what to buy, which politicians to support, and where to vacation," according to Ed Keller and Jon Berry, authors of the book, *The Influentials*. Normally, 10% of Americans qualify as Influentials. Our study found that 69% of Online Political Citizens are Influentials.[15]

Thus, although OPCs make up approximately seven percent of the American population, they exert a disproportionate "multiplier effect" on the public at large. The study speculates that the OPCs of 2004 are "harbingers of permanent change in American politics."

A critical feature of online citizenship is that it is *participatory*. Online citizens are not passive consumers of whatever the political parties are marketing. "Old" politics is conducted within a pyramid— the elite are at the top, disseminating philosophies and policies and candidates to the masses below.

But web politics are *spherical*. Stirling Newberry, a contributor to The Blogging of the President and other blogs, referenced Ralph Waldo Emerson's essay "Circles" as a key to understanding politics on the web. "That's the image you should have of what's happening on the Internet," Newberry said. "Anyone on any given day can be the center if he has the best observation that resonates. There is no boundary of the circle... You get to sing a song and listen to the echo. You get to hear... how other people have taken what you've done and turned it into their center."[16]

Will old-style, Big Media campaign managers adjust to web politics? Doing so will mean giving up their power to frame arguments and control messages. It will not be a smooth transition. But if not this year, then eventually, the web will rival television as a medium of political power.

The Post-Media Age

Just as the Dean campaign found a way to bypass the old power structures, so are increasing numbers of people bypassing traditional media for political news and commentary.

> The Internet reveals the moral bankruptcy of the political journalists like George Will and Bob Novak, who have now become as much a part of the system as they were never supposed to be. Instead of scrupulously guarding against conflicts of interest, there's a carnival-like race towards best-selling agenda-laden punditry and consulting.[17]
>
> —Matt Stoller, The Blogging of the President
> (www.bopnews.com)

To many, the "pundits" who dominate political dialogue in major news media seem to be nothing but shills for the Washington power elite. And when every radio and cable 24-hour news network runs incessant, identical coverage of Michael Jackson, Kobe Bryant, or another celebrity *du jour*, the audience for "hard" news is relying more and more on the Internet. Pent-up frustration with what passes for "journalism" met new web technologies—and writers and readers of blogs came together.

Frank Rich of the *New York Times* is one of the few old-technology journalists to have glimpsed the revolution, and he sent a warning to his colleagues that they are unprepared for the Internet's growing influence. He compared the reaction of television correspondents to web political movements like the Dean campaign with the party scene in the film "Singin' in the Rain," "where Hollywood's silent-era elite greets the advent of talkies with dismissive bafflement."[18]

Big Media and other institutions of political authority are not going away, of course. But, says Dan Gillmore of the *San Jose Mercury-News*, we can look forward to "a diffusion of some information, and some power, an inexorable democratization (small 'd'). There won't be an obvious turning point, but someday we'll look back and say, 'Wow, something really has changed.'"[19]

The revolution is just starting. Remarkable things could happen in the next few years.

Endnotes

[1] Some prominent bloggers are known only by pseudonyms.

[2] Oliver Burkeman, "Bloggers Catch What *Washington Post* Missed," *The Guardian*, December 21, 2002.

[3] See, for example, Melanie Sloan, "Whatever Happened to the Plame Investigation," Buzzflash.com, December 10, 2003 (www.buzzflash.com/contributors/03/12/con03369.html).

[4] Rebecca Blood, *The Weblog Handbook* (Perseus, 2002), p. 2.

[5] Interview with Christopher Lydon, July 31, 2003 (http://blogs.law.harvard.edu/lydon/2003/07/31#a213).

[6] Jay Rosen, "Press Think," TomPaine.com, January 22, 2004 (www.tompaine.com/feature2.cfm/ID/9814).

[7] Kay McFadden, "Dismal Iowa Caucus Coverage Was Just the Tip of the Iceberg," *The Seattle Times*, January 24, 2004.

[8] Rebecca Blood, *The Weblog Handbook* (Perseus, 2002), p. 23.

[9] Kevin Drum, "Blogs vs. Newspapers," Calpundit, January 21, 2004. (http://www.calpundit.com/archives/003093.html).

[10] Jay Rosen, "Private Life, Public Happiness and the Howard Dean Connection," *Pressthink*, December 9, 2003.

[11] Rosen, *ibid.*

[12] Christopher Lydon, "Dick Morris: An Entirely New Age in American Politics," *The Blogging of the President: 2004*, December 11, 2003.

[13] Speech at O'Reilly's Digital Democracy Teach-In, San Diego, CA, Feb. 9–10, 2004 (http://www.itconversations.com/transcript.php?id=80).

[14] Scott Rosenberg, "Politics by Other Means," Salon, Feb. 4, 2004 (www.salon.com/tech/col/rose/2004/02/10/democracy/index.html).

[15] "Political Influentials Online in the 2004 Presidential Campaign," The Graduate School of Policy Management, The George Washington University, Washington, DC, released February 5, 2004 (www.ipdi.org/Influentials/Report.pdf).

[16] "Pyramid and Sphere: Stirling Newberry," interview with Christopher Lydon, Oct. 28, 2003 (http://blogs.law.harvard.edu/lydon/2003/10/28#a399).

[17] Matt Stoller, "A Response to Jay Rosen," The Blogging of the President 2004 (BOPNews), December 23, 2004 (http://www.bopnews.com/archives/000105.html#000105).

[18] Frank Rich, "Napster Runs for President," *The New York Times*, December 21, 2003 (www.nytimes.com/2003/12/21/arts/21RICH.html?ei=5007&en=035abc452122c4ec&ex=1387342800).

[19] Ed Gillmore, "Internet Emerging as a Political Force," *The San Jose Mercury-News*, Jan. 21, 2004 (www.mercurynews.com/mld/mercurynews/business/7759804.htm).

Web Sites Referenced in This Chapter

The Blogging of the President (BOP News)—www.bopnews.com

Calpundit—www.washingtonmonthly.com, formerly www.calpundit.com

Eschaton—www.atrios.blogspot.com

Instapundit—www.instapundit.com

The Mahablog—www.mahablog.com

Pressthink—http://journalism.nyu.edu/pubzone/weblogs/pressthink

Talking Points Memo—www.talkingpointsmemo.com

CHAPTER 2

Charting the Blogosphere
Part 1: The Right Blogosphere

◆━━◆━━◆━━◆━━◆

WEBLOGS HAVE GROWN in number from a few hundred in the late 1990s to a few thousand in 2000 to *a lot more* by 2004. Technorati, a blog search engine, claims to be "watching" 1,543,623 blogs as I write this. Of these, however, *only* thousands are primarily political.

For a technical entity, the blogosphere seems remarkably organic. Every day new blogs are added and deleted. Sites are abandoned and left to decay—links breaking one by one—while other sites thrive and grow.

Like any social creature, bloggers build relationships with each other. They link to and promote other blogs they admire. They organize themselves around special interests. Some blogs form a nexus from which readers spin off other blogs. The result is often compared to an ecosystem, although it might also be compared to the cosmos. Bloggers form galaxies and solar systems, and one could argue there are asteroids, shooting stars, and black holes as well.

Politically partisan divisions exist on the web just as they exist in the flesh-and-blood world. And, as in the non-virtual world, political opinions are continually in flux. Trying to grasp what the blogosphere "thinks" on any issue seems as futile as scooping up the ocean in a butterfly net.

Let's try it, anyway. But please understand that all we can do is examine the creature as it was at a particular moment in time. By the time this is published, much will have changed. Also note that there are hundreds, if not thousands, of blogs making a real contribution to our national political dialogue. I can survey only a few.

The Right Blogosphere

The Ur-Web Site for many conservatives is Free Republic (www. freerepublic.com), created and operated by a programmer named James Robinson of Fresno, California. The story of Free Republic—how it started and grew, and where it is now—is as good as any to illustrate the nature and origins of the Right Blogosphere.

Long, long ago, before the Internet became accessible to people who didn't speak Unix, there were dial-up services like CompuServe and Prodigy. James Robinson got started as a political commentator by writing on the Prodigy bulletin boards in the early 1990s. He also became active on Usenet, a pre-web byway of the Internet. And as the World Wide Web was taking off in the mid-1990s, Robinson wrote his own web-based bulletin board software and launched Free Republic.

The original Free Republic went online in September 1996 as an open forum for discussion of conservative politics. It soon became a cauldron of opposition to President William J. Clinton. Discussion, scandals, rumors, humor, and outright derision came together to create a distinct online culture and something of a movement. Free Republic regulars called themselves "Freepers." The site enabled like-minded conservatives to find each other, share opinions and information, and even organize into state chapters.

Freepers created new web sites, mostly archives of information on Clinton-related scandals and collections of (mostly bawdy) Clinton-related graphical humor. One such site, the BeachBum's Clinton Scandal Page (users.aol.com/beachbt), appears to have been a real political blog. BBCSP went online in 1996 (which would make it among the earliest political blogs) and featured short personal observations from Mr. Bum and links to news articles. The site was abandoned in 2000, leaving an animated .GIF of Janet Reno gesticulating ceaselessly to the few who find her.

Although Free Republic itself is not a blog, it was a platform from which many conservatives found their online voices and went on to blogging. Further, love them or hate them, Freepers are an undeniably large presence on the web. (Online citizens of the Left use the word *Freeper* or *Freep* as a pejorative to describe all perceived barking moonbats of the Right.)

The Drudge Report (www.drudgereport.com) remains one of the most frequently visited political sites on the web. The proprietor, Matt Drudge, publishes links to news stories around the web and originates news as well. Drudge began his career as a one-man news bureau in 1994 by posting messages to Usenet, and his web site went online in 1995. He quickly became famous—or infamous, depending on your political preferences—as a purveyor of news, gossip, and rumor of the many scandals surrounding President Clinton.

For example, *Newsweek* and other "old" media organizations sat on the Monica Lewinsky "blue dress" story until January 1998, when Drudge reported both the story and a *Newsweek* decision to spike it. Quickly the "old" media published the story. Of this episode, journalist Michael Kinsley wrote, "Clinterngate, or whatever we are going to call it, is to the Internet what the Kennedy assassination was to TV news: its coming of age as a media force."[1]

Here is the Saga of the Dress, in brief. On Jan. 21, 1998, Matt Drudge reported the existence of a cocktail dress owned by Ms. Lewinsky that was stained with evidence of the intern's affair with the President. "I know it to be a black cocktail dress," Drudge said, although he wouldn't say exactly where he got his information. (Later accounts described the dress as blue.) The next day Drudge was interviewed about the dress by Matt Lauer on NBC's Today show, thus giving the story mainstream legitimacy.

Although many complained that Drudge was just a gossip monger, Columbia Journalism School dean Tom Goldstein defended Drudge. "Matt Drudge in this case is a legitimate news source," Goldstein said. "He's part of the story." [2]

Not all of Matt Drudge's scoops are so fortuitous. In 1997 he claimed in an "exclusive" that an unnamed source in the Republican Party possessed "court records" documenting violence by White House aide Sidney Blumenthal against his wife. Blumenthal promptly slapped Drudge with a $30 million lawsuit. Drudge retracted the story, but an outraged Blumenthal pressed ahead with the suit until both parties agreed to drop the litigation and settle in May 2001.

More recently, Drudge picked up a press corps rumor alleging an affair between Senator John Kerry, a candidate for the Democratic presidential nomination in 2004, and a young woman on his staff. Major media dutifully repeated the story, albeit with a great many qualifiers. As I write, the Associated Press reports that the young woman denies the allegations. But it put Drudge back in the news.

Glenn Reynolds, a law professor at the University of Tennessee, maintains two very successful blogs—Instapundit (www.instapundit.com), his original site, and GlennReynolds.com (www.msnbc.msn.com/id/3395977/), which is sponsored by Microsoft Network (MSN).[3] It must be noted that Reynolds himself does not like to be pigeonholed as a conservative. He sides with liberals on many social issues, such as gay marriage and legal abortion, he points out. Even so, on balance Instapundit is a politically conservative blog that stands behind the Bush Administration most of the time. In particular, Reynolds is chief among the warbloggers—bloggers who support the Bush Administration's decision to invade Iraq.

Reynolds says he stumbled into blogging. "I teach Internet law and I like to do new and different stuff on the web, and I was looking for something new and different to do, and I was an admirer of Mickey Kaus[4] ... so as a result I decided to start a blog and I thought it would do well if I could get a couple of hundred people to read it."[5] Today Reynolds's circulation exceeds 100,000 hits a day.

"I sit at my computer and I type stuff," he told an interviewer. "I go about my fairly ordinary life out in flyover country, and I just do my thing."[6] Or, as Andrew Sullivan described him, Reynolds is "a hyperactive law professor who churns out dozens of posts a day and has quickly become a huge presence in opinion journalism."[7]

Instapundit is a "classic" blog—short commentaries are posted throughout the day, with new posts on top and old posts sinking to the bottom and eventually to the archives. A column to the left of the comments contains ads, links, and a blogroll.

Like Glenn Reynolds, Steven C. Den Beste, also known as the Captain of the U.S.S. Clueless (that's a starship blog, not an ocean-going vessel—denbeste.nu) is uncomfortable with the label "conservative." He described his political worldview in February 2003:

I am a humanist. I am a liberal, in the classic sense of the term, meaning that I think that the goal of a political system should be to liberate the individuals within it to have as much ability to make decisions about their own lives as is practical, with as little interference by other citizens or the mechanisms of the state. I strongly believe in diversity at every level: diversity of opinions, diversity of political beliefs, diversity of lifestyles. When in doubt, permit it unless it is clearly a danger to the survival of the state or threatens the health and wellbeing of those within the state.

Which, in 2003 in the United States, makes me a "conservative," at least in the reckoning of self-anointed "Liberals" in this nation. I've never been comfortable with that term, myself, and indeed I'm uncomfortable with almost any "ism" as a label for my beliefs (except for "humanism" and "populism"). Is there such a thing as "ain'tism", as in "I ain't any ism"?

Part of why I'm uncomfortable being labeled "conservative" is that those who categorize me in that way then group me with many other "conservatives" with whom I deeply and fundamentally disagree, and try to pretend that I must agree with them and defend them and partake of their attitudes. For instance, it's hard to see how I could disagree more strongly with anyone than I do with the so-called "Christian Right", as epitomized by Jerry Falwell and Pat Robertson. With their belief that we should establish the US as a Christian theocracy, and their desire to use the legal system to enforce orthodox behavior and punish sinful lifestyles, not to mention their wish to use the school system as an extension of the church to indoctrinate all children, I oppose their programs as strongly as I possibly can. I have been opposed to Falwell as long as I've known about his political agenda.

But part of why I get labeled that way by leftists is because I believe in private property, and because I oppose the use of taxation as a way of legally compelling redistribution of wealth. Like nearly everything else, my feelings on this are relatively centrist; I don't believe in totally abolishing the "social safety net," for instance, but I strongly disagree with the idea that wealth is automatically sinful. I'm not one to try to abolish taxation, but I view it as a way of raising revenue for legitimate government operations and generally oppose its use as a direct tool of social engineering.

Equally, I get labeled as "conservative" because I am unashamedly patriotic. I do not think that my nation is flawless, but on balance I would much rather be a citizen of the US than of any other nation I know of, past or present, and I strongly support my nation. I think the US has done much that is wrong, but I think we've done a lot more right than wrong. All other things being equal, I'd like my nation to continue to exist and to prosper. I certainly have no sympathy at all for the Chomskyite idea that the US is the root of all that is evil in the world today, and thus ultimately even responsible for the attack in September 2001.[8]

NZ Bear of The Truth Laid Bear ("A bear, the world, and a strong urge to hibernate"—www.truthlaidbear.com) is "a software development manager with delusions of journalism." The Bear prefers to use a pseudonym to maintain his family's privacy. Along with Glenn Reynolds and Steven C. Den Beste, the Bear is also a prominent warblogger. In his manifesto "The Bear Doctrine," written in 2002 before the invasion of Iraq, he said,

The days when a nation such as ours could afford to leave hostile enemies alone, simply because they posed no immediate threat to us, are over. We cannot allow any government to remain in power that will harbor terrorists, because even one such nation is sufficient to provide a base of operations that can allow such a group to inflict mass casualties across the globe.

This problem is not going to get better. The depravity and sorrow of September 11th was prelude; it was the beginning, not the end.

It is going to get much, much worse. Imagine for a moment the weapons that will exist, and will be available to terrorists like al Qaeda, fifty years from now. I have no way of predicting precisely what they will be, but I will sadly stand by a prediction that they will be capable of inflicting horrors that are beyond our worst nightmares today.

I wish with all my heart that I turn out to be wrong about this. I would pray for my own foolishness to be revealed, if I knew how.

We have to fix this planet. Now. And it has to be us—America—because nobody else has the power, nor the will.[9]

This is as good a synopsis of the warblogger argument as any I have found. If subsequent events have given the Bear second thoughts, he hasn't written about them.

Most conservative blogs are caught up in U.S. election politics and support the Bush Administration, but there are exceptions. LewRockwell is a popular group blog attached to a libertarian web site. Editor-in-chief Llewellyn Rockwell calls himself "an opponent of the central state, its wars and its socialism." LewRockwell publishes both short comments and essays by a number of contributors that focus on political philosophy rather than political parties. When LewRockwell essays do discuss political parties, there is no apparent favoritism—all parties are disparaged equally.

The LewRockwell blog exemplifies something the web does much better than print media—enable public discussion of ideas and worldviews that might be considered out of the mainstream.

In a recent essay Rockwell celebrated the libertarian nature of the web itself. When publishing meant print, people with unconventional political ideas struggled to get articles through editors and placed in newspaper and journals. And even when an article was published, the author had no connection to reader reaction. But web publishing is entirely different. "The really big change has been to bring producers of opinion together with consumers of opinion," Rockwell said.

> I started, during the war on Serbia, to share interesting links with friends," he wrote. "But then my own personal email list became too long. It occurred to me that perhaps people I don't know might be interested in these links. Thus was born my public site, just an interface to display things I saw (this was pre-blog). Then I started publishing people's thoughts, my own thoughts, and the next thing I know, I'm the editor of one of the most trafficked centers of political and economic opinion in the world.[10]

If LewRockwell's thoughtful, scholarly essays stand at one end of a tastefulness scale, The Anti-Idiotarian Rottweiler is close to the other. Boldly calling itself "The most annoying right-of-center blog of 2003," and "Affiliate of the VRWC [Vast Right-Wing Conspiracy]," The Rottweiler is a blog on which punches are not pulled and words are not minced. (Please see Chapter 3, page 92, for an example of Anti-Idiotarian rhetoric.)

Rottweiler's proprietor, the Emperor Misha I (one suspects this is a pseudonym) says in his blog's FAQ, "This is NOT a Family Oriented blog. I happen to LIKE colorful invective and I'm incredibly sick and tired of the PC society we've created in which you have to guard your every word for fear that you might upset somebody and hurt their wittle feewings." So there.

The Emperor started blogging in 2002, but says he'd been reading blogs for quite some time before that. "I've been reading columnists and news sites like crazy since I don't know when, gobbling up opinion and news like it was nobody's business. I guess you might call me a 'news junkie.' But it was a left-wing blog that pulled him into blogging.

> One of the more ridiculous sites on "the other side" (and they aren't all, there are quite a few "Left Wing" sites that I enjoy reading immensely, whether I agree

or not) was called "warbloggerwatch" and was (and is) home to a bunch of tinfoiled loons convinced that everything that ever happened is a result of some sinister Right Wing Conspiracy, something I find wildly amusing.

So I started rebutting their posts in their comments, using the now well-known "Fisking Technique"[11] that I, by the way, DIDN'T invent. :-)

After a while, other readers and posters there started asking me if I'd ever thought about setting up a blog of my own, and the more they pushed, the more I thought "well, why not? I might as well post my material on my own site since I'm posting anyway, and it looks like there are people who'd actually read it," until I finally gave in and set up a blog on "Blogspot."[12]

The Emperor is a supporter of President Bush, for the most part, although he is capable of breaking ranks. He wrote on February 10, 2004, "Apart from his stellar performance on the tax cuts, bringing the economy back from the dead in record time and his kicka** attitude against the swine that attacked us on 9/11/01, he's been doing all that he can lately to talk himself out of a job. Scary if it's true."[13] Although he often calls knee-jerk apologists for Bush "Kool-Aiders," the Emperor prefers President Bush to any Democratic contender.

This brings me to a phenomenon spreading throughout the Right Blogosphere as I write (but which may have reversed itself by the time you read this). As a rule, the rhetoric on most conservative sites rings with *moral clarity*—the bloggers are absolutely certain they know who is right, who is wrong, who is worthy of praise, and who is deserving of derision. Generally, liberal bloggers are more likely to see shades of gray. But at this moment in time I find conservative site after site that is oddly subdued. Some bloggers who used to be fire-breathing, Clinton-bashing, Bush-loving, Lefty-baiting Freepers seem ambivalent about the Bush Administration.

Time and time again, I run into two themes:

> ► Bush is not reducing the size of government, but making it bigger.

► Bush's "immigration" proposal will ruin America (or, at least, mess it up some).

Examples: Little Green Footballs[14] worries that we're trading away too many personal liberties for the sake of security. And View from the Right[15] predicts that "Karl Rove's amnesty plan will be Bush's undoing."

Please note that none of these bloggers appears to be considering supporting any candidate other than George W. Bush in the fall. Further, they continue to give their unstinting support for the U.S. military action in Iraq. But if bloggers are harbingers of anything, the White House should be worried.

Conservative journalist and blogger Andrew Sullivan, senior editor of *New Republic*, author, and frequent cable television guest pundit may be suffering a crisis of conscience also. On his blog AndrewSullivan, the gay Mr. Sullivan broke ranks with the White House on the issue of gay marriage and is embarrassed by the failure to find weapons of mass destruction in Iraq. In one widely circulated essay, "Nanny in Chief: Bush Versus Freedom,"[16] Sullivan despairs that the Bush Administration is pushing a big-government, anti-libertarian agenda. "He is fusing big government liberalism with religious Right moralism," said Sullivan. Yet as of this writing Sullivan remains in Bush's camp.

While researching this chapter I spent most of my time looking at high-traffic, frequently linked blogs. It's simple to find where web traffic is going by checking with web service providers like Technorati (www.technorati.com) or Alexa (www.alexa.com). And if traffic is an indicator, the majority of web conservatives align themselves with a position that might be called "muscular libertarianism." These bloggers are capable of breaking ranks with the hard right on many social issues, such as gay rights, mostly on libertarian grounds—some things just aren't the government's business. Some worry that Attorney General John Ashcroft is a threat to their personal liberty, although they like his defense of their Second Amendment right to own firearms. They seem to have little affinity with the Religious Right. But they support the Bush Administration in most things, especially the war in Iraq. They see American military aggression as the chief tool to protect Americans from terrorists. And they are contemptuous of Democrats, who are believed to be uninterested in national security. Further, conventional wisdom on the right says a Democratic-controlled federal government would tax working Americans into poverty for the sake of social welfare programs.

Blogs that more or less reflect this point of view are the ones that make all the "top traffic" lists—e.g., GlennReynolds, AndrewSullivan, VodkaPundit, U.S.S. Clueless. Glenn Reynolds may argue that his blog is not conservative, but it appears that on the web it exemplifies the majority conservative view. There *are* social conservatives blogging in favor of prayer in school and against gay marriage and legal abortion, but the bulk of web traffic is passing them by. "Hard" right positions mostly are disseminated from web sites that don't allow comments or encourage feedback.

From a liberal blogger, some concluding observations of the right:

Bloggers of the right often conflate "liberal" with "socialist" and have bought into the belief that "liberals" cannot be patriots. Certainly there are American liberals who are unabashedly patriotic—I'm one— and who support capitalism even while criticizing its excesses. It may be that, if we can get past stereotypes and propaganda and semantic confusion, Right and Left are not as far apart as we all believe. If so, maybe in the future we can find common ground in the Blogosphere. We are a long way from that now, however.

In the 1990s sites like Drudge Report and Free Republic flamed with antipathy toward President Clinton. The Clinton scandals fanned the flames, and bloggers like Drudge did their part to keep scandals in the headlines. I cannot say whether the web helped drive the impeachment of President Clinton in 1998; the impeachment may have happened web or no web. However, in those years the Right Blogosphere became part of a vast echo chamber of right-wing views, made up of news sources (e.g., Fox News, Clear Channel radio, *The Weekly Standard*), politicians, and political operatives.

Those inside the echo chamber see it as an oasis of truth in a desert of liberal propaganda. To those of us on the outside, the echo chamber seems a closed and impenetrable system in which the World According to Rush Limbaugh has replaced objective reality. In any case, it appears that mass media are being replaced by politically targeted media, a phenomenon that bears watching.

Right-wing bloggers overall (not necessarily the bloggers surveyed in this chapter) have a dreary tendency to use the adjectives *liberal* or *lefty* as pejoratives to describe any political position the blogger does not like. The actual definitions of *liberalism* as a political philosophy and the distinctions between *liberal* and *leftist* are utterly lost, just as (I admit) the distinctions between *conservative* and *right wing* are often lost on liberal blogs.

In particular, it is common to associate "liberalism" with "big government programs that waste money." A survey of bloggings about the excesses of President Bush's proposed 2005 budget unearthed comments that his out-of-control spending made Bush a "liberal" or that he was turning to the "Left." One expects to turn a corner and find Alice addressing Humpty Dumpty:

> "When *I* use a word," Humpty Dumpty said, in rather a scornful tone, "it means just what I choose it to mean— neither more nor less."
>
> "The question is," said Alice "whether you *can* make words mean so many different things."
>
> "The question is," said Humpty Dumpty, "which is to be master—that's all."[17]

I am personally distressed at the common notions that liberals do not love America, or that we don't care about national security, or that we don't understand the significance of September 11. I was in lower Manhattan on September 11 and witnessed the collapse of the World Trade Center towers. It is an event burned into my brain. If you weren't there, may I suggest you don't understand it as I do.

And on September 13 I came back to Manhattan. I felt compelled just to walk about and look at the city, my adopted city, to reassure myself it was still there. As I stood on 42nd Street and looked up and down Madison Avenue, I saw flags, beautiful American flags, swaying from flagpoles and draped from windows.

I've read that in the Civil War the flag bearers on the battlefield had an absurdly high mortality rate—they'd be the first ones shot. Yet when a flag bearer fell, another soldier always would take up the flag. I think now I know why.

Right and left can disagree on the *means* of protecting the nation from terrorism, but as long as the right equates disagreement with *its* policy ideas with being unpatriotic or soft on terrorism, we will continue to talk past each other.

◆——◆——◆——◆——◆——◆

Endnotes

[1] Michael Kinsley, "In Defense of Matt Drudge," *Time*, February 2, 1998.

[2] Adam Cohen, "The Press and The Dress," *Time*, February 16, 2004.

[3] To read this blog, go to MSN (www.msnbc.msn.com/id/3395977/).

[4] Mickey Kaus's very conservative political blog is sponsored on MSN.

[5] Interview with Christopher Lydon, July 31, 2003 (http://blogs.law.harvard.edu/lydon/2003/07/31#a213).

[6] *Ibid.*

[7] Andrew Sullivan, "The Blogging Revolution," *Wired*, May 2002.

[8] http://denbeste.nu/cd_log_entries/2003/02/LiberalConservatism.shtml.

[9] www.truthlaidbear.com/archives/2002/07/31/foreign_policy_ttlb_stylethe_bear_doctrine.php.

[10] Llewellyn H. Rockwell, Jr., "And the Word Was Made Web," LewRockwell, February 5, 2004 (www.lewrockwell.com/rockwell/Web.html).

[11] The blog Volokh Conspiracy for August 2, 2002, defines *fisking*: "The term refers to Robert Fisk, a journalist who wrote some rather foolish anti-war stuff, and who in particular wrote a story in which he (1) recounted how he was beaten by some anti-American Afghan refugees, and (2) thought they were morally right for doing so. Hence many pro-war blogs—most famously, InstaPundit—often use the term "Fisking" figuratively to mean *a thorough and forceful verbal beating of an anti-war, possibly anti-American, commentator who has richly earned this figurative beating through his words.* Good Fisking tends to be (or at least aim to be) quite logical, and often quotes the other article in detail, interspersing criticisms with the original article's text." (Eugene Volokh).

[12] Email to the author, February 12, 2004.

[13] Archived at www.nicedoggie.net/archives/003742.html#003742.

[14] http://littlegreenfootballs.com/weblog/?entry=9749_Slouching_Toward_Big_Brother.

[15] www.amnation.com/vfr/archives/002162.html.

[16] Published in the January 24, 2004 issue of Time magazine and on his blog at www.andrewsullivan.com/main_article.php?artnum=20040126.

[17] Lewis Carroll, *Through the Looking Glass.*

Web Sites Referenced in This Chapter

AndrewSullivan—www.andrewsullivan.com

Anti-Idolitarian Rottweiler—www.nicedoggie.net

The Drudge Report—www.drudgereport.com

Free Republic—www.freerepublic.com

Instapundit—www.instapundit.com

LewRockwell—http://blog.lewrockwell.com

Little Green Footballs—www.littlegreenfootballs.com/weblog/weblog.php

The Truth Laid Bear—www.truthlaidbear.com

U.S.S. Clueless—http://denbeste.nu

View from the Right—http://amnation.com/vfr

VodkaPundit—www.vodkapundit.com

Charting the Blogosphere
Part 2: The Left Blogosphere

––––––◆–◆–◆–◆–◆––––––

WITH A FEW NOTABLE EXCEPTIONS such as Bartcop (www.bartcop. com), online since 1996, the Left was underrepresented on the web during the Clinton Administration. Then came the Bush Administration, and suddenly the Left had something to blog about. After the 2000 Florida vote fiasco, liberal blogs blossomed like flowers in spring, or algae in a pond, depending on your political preferences.

As I write, the collective will of the entire Left Blogosphere is focused on the November 2004 presidential election. Although there are as many unique perspectives on this as there are bloggers, the desire to see President Bush defeated and out of the White House trumps them all. To this end, liberal bloggers not only criticize the Bush Administration; they also expose the faults and biases of old-media campaign coverage and mobilize supporters of Democratic candidates.

For example, in February 2004 a Democratic candidate for U.S. Congress achieved victory through blogs. A special election for an empty seat in Kentucky's sixth district saw Democrat Ben Chandler running against Republican state Senator Alice Kerr. Two weeks before the election, Kerr had used a million dollar war chest to close Chandler's once-sizable lead. Chandler didn't have the campaign cash to mount a counter-offensive.

But Chandler's campaign manager, Mark Nicholas, decided to try something new. He used $2,000 to buy ad space on 11 mostly liberal blogs such as Daily Kos (www.dailykos.com) and Eschaton (http:// atrios.blogspot.com). Nicholas hoped that the blogs would reach

Democrats who would contribute to keeping a Democratic seat in Congress.

In two weeks, the $2,000 investment returned more than $80,000 in campaign contributions, enabling the campaign to buy more radio and cable television ads. And Ben Chandler won the election. Wrote Josh Marshall of Talking Points Memo (www.talkingpointsmemo.com):

> This was the first federal election of the 2004 cycle. Kerr based her campaign almost exclusively on her strong support for the Bush agenda. And the AP is now reporting that Chandler has beaten Kerr decisively. That marks the first time since 1991 that a Democrat has won a Republican seat in a special election.[1]

Naturally, other Democratic candidates are now buying blog space for ads. Chandler's success may not be duplicated, however, since Chandler had the field of donors to himself. Further, support from the blogs went beyond just advertising. Some bloggers—notably Markos Zúniga of Daily Kos—also blogged their support for Chandler, arguing that Democrats around the country had a stake in the race. Now that the sidebars of many liberal blogs are filled with campaign ads, the candidates are competing for dollars and the attention of the bloggers.

Still, ads on blogs appear to be a good way for candidates to target like-minded potential donors and campaign volunteers. And as of this writing, campaign blog ad buyers are almost all Democrats; Republicans appear to remain skeptical about the impact of blogs. Larry Purpuro, coordinator of the Republicans' e.GOP Project in 2000, dismissed bloggers as "armchair analysts in their bathrobes (with) no serious interest in leaving their living rooms to actually help the campaigns."[2] We'll see.

But before there were campaign ads on blogs, there was Media Whores Online (MWO, www.mediawhoresonline.com) and other sites dedicated to old media criticism. Disgruntled—to say the least—with the quality of political news reporting, much of the Left Blogosphere focuses on the faults of old media nearly as much as on politics. MWO and The Blogging of the President (www.bopnews.com) have asked readers to choose one reporter or pundit to blog about to ensure depth of coverage. Many liberal bloggers publish examples of media bias or just plain bad reporting and encourage readers to write, fax, phone, or email news organizations to complain. Whether blogging will effect substantive improvement in political reporting remains to be seen, however.

In spite of their possibly growing clout, many liberal bloggers still feel outnumbered. "There are two times as many Republican blogs as there are Democratic blogs," says Mary Beth Williams of Wampum. "In part that's because there are more Republicans online than Democrats because Republicans have more money."[3] Meaning, money to buy computers, Internet access, and bandwidth.

I have no hard data comparing numbers of liberal versus conservative blogs, so I can't say if the perception of fewer liberal than conservative blogs is true. Even so, there are more "best" liberal blogs than I can possibly survey in one chapter. What follows is a selective and subjective tour of popular liberal blogs.

Joshua Micah Marshall launched Talking Points Memo at the beginning of the Florida 2000 election fiasco, making TPM one of the oldest liberal blogs. It's also among the most successful political blogs. In February 2004, the site had 2,192,404 page views, 1,632,034 visits and 411,239 individual visitors.[4]

Marshall has a foot in both old and new media. He is a contributing writer on politics, culture, and foreign affairs for *Washington Monthly* and a columnist for *The Hill,* a weekly newspaper reporting on the inner workings of Congress. He has also turned up on television political talk shows such as CNN's "Crossfire" and MSNBC's "Hardball."

In an interview with Kevin Drum, formerly of Calpundit (www.calpundit.com) and now of Political Animal (www .washingtonmonthly.com), Marshall said he writes TPM because he enjoys being able to speak his mind without the constraints of writing for a magazine or newspaper. He rationalized his non-paid work on TPM by thinking of it as a loss-leader for his professional writing career. "And to a great degree," he said, "it turned out to be true."[5]

Marshall also believes that blogs are where talk radio was a few years ago, evolving into a significant force before being recognized as such. And it's a force that, for some reason, works particularly well for Democrats. Marshall pointed out in a February blog that Republicans have always been better than Democrats at raising money through direct mail. This is partly because of better mailing lists and partly because the GOP demographic responds better to direct mail than Democrats do. But the Internet seems to work well for Democrats, "allowing them to raise large sums of money, not from a few well-heeled givers but from large numbers of energized Democrats giving $10, $50, or $100 a shot. It's already starting to make a difference."[6]

Eschaton (www.atrios.blogspot.com) went online April 17, 2002, with a simple message: "Is this thing on?" Followed by, "I wonder how long it will be until literally dozens of people are reading this on an almost monthly basis." Since that day, the site has received more than 11 million hits. Currently Eschaton averages 40,000 hits per day.

The proprietor is a 30-something man from Philadelphia, rumored to be a public school teacher, who goes by the name Atrios. Like many bloggers, Atrios got into writing on the web through an online forum, in this case *Salon*'s Table Talk. The name "Eschaton" comes from a passage in the novel *Infinite Jest* by David Foster Wallace. In the novel, Eschaton is the name of a complicated and chaotic game played by students at a private tennis academy.

A profile of Atrios in the March 2004 issue of *Philadelphia* magazine describes the blogger watching the Iowa caucus returns in a Philadelphia bar: "The most powerful person in the room may be the man in the turtleneck sweater. And no one knows who the hell he is."[7] Powerful? For example, Atrios was instrumental in the resignation of Trent Lott as Senate Majority Leader (see Chapter 1).

Regarding anonymity—Atrios is far from the only anonymous blogger in the Blogosphere. Even so, at times his anonymity has become an issue. For example, in October 2003, *National Review* columnist Donald Luskin threatened Atrios with a libel lawsuit for calling Luskin a "stalker," which seemed peculiar because Atrios merely had linked a Luskin column in which Luskin called himself a stalker.[8] But the legal action, which would have put Atrios's real name in public record, was resolved outside of court.

Also, conservative blogger Andrew Sullivan criticized Atrios in a January 2004 radio interview, saying his anonymity violates a basic tenet of the blogosophere—transparency. But another blogger, Charles Kuffner of Off the Kuff, pointed out that Atrios's identity is irrelevant because he makes no claims of insider knowledge or special expertise.

Which is why the other recent brouhaha, about Atrios's secret identity, is so much baloney. Can you think of any single thing that Atrios has posted where one needs to accept that he does in fact have access to information that you don't? I can't. Atrios deals in publicly available data, stuff that anyone could find. Surely by now if his identity were material to his blogging, someone would have pointed to one or more of his posts and asked "How do you know that? What is your source?" If you mentally substitute "Dominic Scarpetti", or "Jerome Horwitz", or "Yon Yonson from Wisconsin" wherever you see the word "Atrios", does it change your perception of the veracity of his words?

But what if he really is Bob Shrum, or Sidney Blumenthal, or (gasp!) HILLARY!?!? Well, then I'd say Atrios has done a better job than Curt Schilling did of not dropping any hints to his identity of the "only a few people could possibly know this" kind over the past few years, going back to his pre-blog Table Talk days, the kind of hints that a Mickey Kaus or Andrew Sullivan could pounce on with a gleeful "Aha!" [Schilling is the Boston Red Sox pitcher who anonymously participated in online chats before signing his current contract.] Indeed, the fact that Sully has no clue who Atrios is after all this time—and remember, we've had the chance to hear Atrios's voice, too—is to me the strongest evidence that his real name wouldn't mean anything to Sully anyway. And if I'm wrong, and Atrios truly is an insider of some kind, he's doing a pretty excellent impersonation of someone who isn't. In either case, who Atrios is has no real bearing on what Atrios says, and that's what really matters.[9]

Bloggers maintain anonymity for many reasons. Political bloggers with strong opinions often prefer that readers at least don't know where they live. Atrios, who admits he has a "public job" in "education," is concerned that celebrity would interfere with his employment.

Daily Kos (www.dailykos.com) went online in April 2002 and currently receives over 2.5 million unique visits per month. Kos is Markos Moulitsas Zúniga, a US Army veteran and lawyer living in San Francisco. Daily Kos qualifies as a group blog, featuring articles from several bloggers plus a "diaries" section where registered members may post articles. Between bloggers and commenters the site is continually updated. You can dip into Daily Kos several times a day and always find something new.

A prominent Kos alumnus is Billmon of the blog Whiskey Bar (www.billmon.org). The anonymous Billmon is a prolific writer who is particularly good at explaining the economy. He revealed in a blog from October 23, 2003, that he is or was a journalist covering U.S. economic issues: "In my own journalistic *first* career, I covered the Clinton economic team for about three years," he wrote. His January blogs from the World Economic Forum at Davos were a blend of personal journal, economic theory and gossip that were more fun to read than any Davos reporting I'd seen in newspapers:

> I'm in Zurich, heading home. It's a gray, solemn European city — looking like what I imagine Munich or Frankfurt or Hamburg would look like if they hadn't been bombed to cinders in World War II. Lots of formal old buildings with heavy Teutonic facades intermingled with newer, modernist office blocks that wouldn't have looked out of place behind the Iron Curtain.
>
> Perhaps because of that—and the old-fashioned trolley cars that run down virtually every main street—the city reminds me vaguely of Moscow: but a clean, well-maintained Moscow, filled with well-dressed, well-fed people. This, of course, is a complete oxymoron. But Zurich does have the same feeling of being a city that is both dowdy and powerful, like an elderly matron with a large family to manage. ...
>
> *Economics.* That's what the forum is *supposed* to be about, although over the years the agenda has broadened to include sessions like this year's "Artists as Fore-

casters of the Future," "Me Inc.," and "Once Upon a Faith." Not surprisingly, the big economic topic this year was the sustainability of the U.S. expansion. Surprisingly, there was a tremendous amount of attention to the enormous U.S. current account deficit, and the downward pressure it is putting on the dollar.

Regulars at Whiskey Bar know these last two topics are, if not dear to my heart, then at least central to my views on the U.S. economy. And yet, I think it's fair to say they hardly ever break the surface of mainstream economic commentary here in the United States, where it's generally taken for granted that Asian central banks will continue to buy enormous quantities of dollars and U.S. Treasury securities ad infinitum, allowing America to simultaneously finance a huge federal budget deficit, a capital spending boom and a steadily rising standard of living, despite having the lowest savings rate of any advanced industrial nation.

This complacency most definitely is not shared by the Europeans, who are watching the rising euro with the same sinking feeling that King Midas must have felt when he realized that everything he touched, including his food, was turning to gold....[10]

While we're discussing economists—Brad DeLong is a professor of economics at the University of California at Berkeley and former Deputy Assistant Secretary of the Treasury who blogs at Brad DeLong's Website (www.j-bradford-delong.net/movable_type), a.k.a. Brad DeLong's Semi-Daily Journal. Like Billmon, Professor DeLong blogs on many aspects of politics and culture, but he *really* cooks when he's talking numbers. Blogs range from serious economic analysis to silliness—for example, from February 26, 2004, some "two cows" jokes:

Parmalat:

You had two cows. But now you don't know where they are.

Pentagon:

Donald Rumsfeld informed the Congress that he had accurate satellite intelligence about where the two cows were. But he lied.[11]

Kevin Drum's *Political Animal* is a personal favorite. Drum is a Silicon Valley marketing consultant with a degree in journalism. His original blog, Calpundit, averaged more than 40,000 page views per day and was known for moderately liberal views and Friday Cat Blogging, the practice of blogging about one's cats on Friday. Drum moved his blogging to Political Animal, which is sponsored by *Washington Monthly* magazine, in March 2004.

Drum offered these observations on blogging on February 20, 2003:

I've also read a lot of old small-town newspapers over the past year as part of my genealogy hobby, and one of the things you immediately notice about them is how raw and unedited they were. It was basically just the editor—who was also publisher, circulation manager, and typesetter—talking to his audience. Television news in 1963 was probably pretty similar: just a camera and a reporter talking about what they saw.

And it occurs to me that this explains some of the popularity of blogs too: the very fact that they aren't professional attracts us. Television, of course, passed the ultra-professional-highly-filtered-snazzy-graphics threshold years ago, and for that reason probably leaves many of us unsatisfied. Not because we think they're deliberately lying to us, but because we instinctively know that their very professionalism gets in the way of *just telling us what's happening.* When every story consists of a fancy graphic and a 45-second spot edited to within an inch of its life, you know that what you're seeing bears the same resemblance to real life that a Playboy centerfold does to the girl next door.

Blogs, of course, don't provide much in the way of original reporting, but they *do* provide us what those

> old small-town newspapers did before they grew up: a
> quick and conversational combination of news, opin-
> ion, gossip, and weird personal idiosyncrasies. It may
> not be pretty, but at least it's real.[12]

There are hundreds of first-rate political blogs, and this book will fail to mention many that some readers consider essential reading. That can't be helped. But I believe if I leave out Hullabaloo (http://digbysblog.blogspot.com) I will never hear the end of it. The anonymous author, known as Digby, is fresh in every sense of the word. Other liberal blogs worthy of note include The Hamster (http://the-hamster.com) and Orcinus (dneiwert.blogspot.com).

Although I don't know if liberals are still underrepresented in the Blogosphere, I can say with some authority that women are. However, there are some outstanding women political bloggers, including Jeanne d'Arc of Body and Soul (bodyandsoul.typepad.com/blog/) Maru at WTF Is It Now? (maruthecrankpot.blogspot.com) and Elayne Riggs of Pen-Elayne on the Web (elayneriggs.blogspot.com).

Earlier I said the Right Blogosphere seemed to be part of closed echo chamber of right-wing opinion. Is the same true of the Left Blogosphere? Perhaps. Here's an observation from my own blog:

> While skipping between right and left blogosphere, one
> can't help but notice the *disconnect.* It's as if bloggers
> of the left and right are commenting on two entirely
> different planets. It isn't just that opinions differ; often
> we don't comment on the same stories. A story picked
> up by one side of the sphere as Greatly Significant may
> be ignored by the other.
>
> For example, there was a great yawning silence on
> the Right about Bob Woodward's new book [*Plan of
> Attack*]. Go to Technorati and search for "Woodward,"
> and mostly lefty blogs come up. (One exception quotes
> Charles Krauthammer saying that Americans prefer
> Bush over Kerry because "Americans are a serious
> people." That Chuckie K. is a hoot!)
>
> On the other hand, the UNSCAM story[13] is all over
> the Right but mostly ignored on the Left. I haven't been

paying much attention to it, either, and don't know how much there is to it. But, clearly, a story about corruption in the UN *vis à vis* Iraq is one that fits nicely into the Right's worldview but seems irrelevant to the Left.

Another example: Last winter a story about people crushed to death by crowds at the Hajj in Mecca was commented upon by every dadblamed right-wing blog I could find. This news was grasped by the Right as just one more example of how substandard those Muslims are (unless they are pro-American Iraqi Muslims, in which case they are at least worthy of our concern; the phrase "White Man's Burden" did come to mind). But this tragedy was pretty much ignored on the Left, possibly because we were wrapped up in the Democratic presidential primaries at the time.

Strange but true.[14]

Blogger Juan Cole of Informed Comment (www.juancole.com/) observed that America has developed a "two-party epistemology."[15] We have entered a Twilight Zone where there are not just opposing political philosophies, but opposing *knowledges*. We do not agree on what is fact or fiction, what is valid or invalid, what is true or false. No wonder political "discussion" these days often amounts to people screaming at each other. Instead of "might makes right," we act as if "volume makes right." But whether the web will lead us out of or further into this wilderness of sophistry remains to be seen.

The Right did not elect me to speak for them, but I imagine they would say blogs on the Left spend too much time digging through the President's past, looking for scandal. And the Left would say that in 2000 the old media didn't do its job, which is to dig beneath the spin and present a complete and honest portrait of those who would be President. And the Right might say that a great many blogs do little more than publish tasteless, juvenile ridicule of the President. To which the Left might reply: Yes. So?

The future direction of the Left Blogosphere may be determined by the outcome of the November 2004 presidential election. A great many high-volume sites, both news sites and blogs, are devoted almost entirely to the faults of the Bush Administration. If the Democrats prevail, news sites such as Bush Watch (www.bushwatch.com), and Smirking Chimp (www.smirkingchimp.com), and blogs such as Sick of Bush (www.sickofbush.blogspot.com) and Dubya's Dayly Diary (www.madkane.com/bush.html) may suddenly be obsolete. Just as many anti-Clinton web sites were abandoned after 2000, so may many anti-Bush sites come to the end of their run.

But most bloggers of the Left will, I suspect, continue to find plenty to blog about no matter who wins the election. Liberals and progressives, long marginalized, are finding in the web a new way to organize, articulate ideas, and impact politics and media. And the web isn't going away after the November elections. Along with activist sites such as Moveon (www.moveon.org), blogs may be just the beginning of a transformation of American politics.

The blogs mentioned in this book, Left or Right, are only a starting point. If you aren't already a blog reader, I urge you to go to any blog mentioned in this book and begin to follow links. You may be surprised and amazed. You may be frightened and alarmed. But you won't be bored.

Endnotes

[1] www.talkingpointsmemo.com/archives/week_2004_02_15.html#002569.

[2] Anick Jesdanun, "Campaign Blogs Question Traditional Media," Associated Press/ *Editor and Publisher*, January 23, 3004.

[3] Alex Irvine, "Candidate Blog," *The Portland Phoenix*, February 27, 2004.

[4] www.talkingpointsmemo.com/archives/week_2004_02_01.html#002511.

[5] Calpundit, February 27, 2004 (www.calpundit.com/archives/000351.html).

[6] Talking Points Memo, February 17, 2004 (www.talkingpointsmemo.com/archives/ week_2004_02_15.html#002569).

[7] Jason Fagone, "The Unknown Blogger," *Philadelphia Magazine*, March 2004.

[8] Donald Luskin, "We Stalked. He Balked," *National Review*, May 7, 2003 (www.nationalreview.com/nrof_luskin/truthsquad050703.asp).

[9] Off the Kuff (a blog), February 12, 2004 (www.offthekuff.com/mt/archives/ 003007.html).

[10] http://billmon.org/archives/000986.html.

[11] www.j-bradford-delong.net/movable_type/2004_archives/000384.html.

[12] www.calpundit.com/archives/000470.html.

[13] The UNSCAMscandal follows corruption in the United Nation's Oil-for-Food program, which was set up to force Saddam Hussein to use oil profits for humanitarian needs. According to the *U.S. News and World Report* (http://www.usnews.com/usnews/issue/archive/040426/20040426044199_brief.php), here's how the scam worked: "Saddam sold oil to his friends and allies around the world at deep discounts. The buyers resold the oil at huge profits. Saddam then got kickbacks of 10 percent from both the oil traders and the suppliers of humanitarian goods."

[14] The Mahablog, April 23, 2004 (http://www.mahablog.com/2004.04.18_arch.html).

[15] April 25, 2004, http://www.juancole.com/.2004_04_01_juancole_archive.html #108287521120764481.

Web Sites Referenced in This Section

Bartcop—www.bartcop.com

The Blogging of the President—www.bopnews.com

Body and Soul—http://bodyandsoul.typepad.com/blog/

Brad DeLong's Semi-Daily Journal—www.j-bradford-delong.net/movable_type

Bush Watch—www.bushwatch.com

Calpundit—www.washingtonmonthly.com, formerly www.calpundit.com

Daily Kos—www.dailykos.com

Dubya's Daily Diary—www.madkane.com/bush.html

Eschaton—http://atrios.blogspot.com

The Hamster—http://the-hamster.com

Hullabaloo—http://digbysblog.blogspot.com

Informed Comment—www.juancole.com

Media Whores Online—www.mediawhoresonline.com

Moveon—www.moveon.org

Off the Kuff—www.offthekuff.com/mt

Orcinus—http://dneiwert.blogspot.com

Pen-Elayne on the Web—http://elayneriggs.blogspot.com

Sick of Bush—www.sickofbush.blogspot.com

The Smirking Chimp—www.smirkingchimp.com

Talking Points Memo—http://talkingpointsmemo.com

Wampum—http://wampum.wabanaki.net

Whiskey Bar—http://billmon.org

WTF Is It Now?—http://maruthecrankpot.blogspot.com

CHAPTER 3

Blogging the Issues
Part 1: The State
of the Union, 2004

━━◆━━◆━━◆━━◆━━◆━━

ON JANUARY 20, 2004, President George W. Bush delivered the annual State of the Union Address. And on January 20 and 21, the State of the Union was blogged.

Blogs offer a glimpse into the nation's reaction to the speech across the political spectrum, through the blogs themselves and blog readers' comments. At times Left and Right seem to have reacted to two different speeches. On the other hand, across the board there was concern about the Bush Administration's out-of-control spending and a consensus that the official response of the Democrats was, well, lame.

A note on context: The SOTU address was delivered just one day after the Iowa Caucus. The third-place Iowa finish of Democrat Howard Dean, a favorite son candidate of the web, was fresh in the minds of bloggers and readers. For this reason, commentary is peppered with references to Howard Dean. Also for this reason, many liberal-leaning bloggers skipped the SOTU altogether in favor of Iowa post-mortems. A few did take it on, however, and conservative-leaning blogs nearly all devoted considerable time to it.

A word comes up occasionally that deserves explanation—*fisking*. At one time the word *fisking* referred to criticism of anti-war commentary; as described in the blog Volokh Conspiracy for August 2, 2002:

> The term refers to Robert Fisk, a journalist who wrote some rather foolish anti-war stuff, and who in particular wrote a story in which he (1) recounted how he was beaten by some anti-American Afghan refugees, and (2) thought they were morally right for doing so. Hence many pro-war blogs—most famously, InstaPundit—often use the term "Fisking" figuratively to mean *a thorough and forceful verbal beating of an anti-war, possibly anti-American, commentator who has richly earned this figurative beating through his words.* Good Fisking tends to be (or at least aims to be) quite logical, and often quotes the other article in detail, interspersing criticisms with the original article's text.
>
> —Eugene Volokh[1]

By 2004 the word *fisking* had broken its tether from the topic of war and was being used to mean any detailed analysis of another's speech or writing. And on January 20 and 21, the State of the Union Address was well and thoroughly *fisked*.

The text of the actual speech appears at the beginning of this chapter, with interspersed commentary from two blogs: one by Stephen Green at VodkaPundit (www.vodkapundit.com/archives/005020.php) and one by Kevin Drum at Calpundit (www.calpundit.com/archives/003087.html). Both bloggers posted commentaries while the speech was still being broadcast. To convey the immediacy of what happened during the State of the Union address—the feeling of an entire country gathered around a TV set and calling out comments—several comments left by readers of VodkaPundit and Calpundit blogs are included here. I have also left in the original time stamps, which correlate to the time zones of the bloggers. Note how quickly blog and comments were written and posted. Also note that some spelling and punctuation were corrected.

Other bloggers featured following the speech include Emporer Misha at Anti-Idiotarian Rotwieller (www.nicedoggie.net/archives/003662.html#003662), David Neiwert at Ornicus (http://dneiwert .blogspot.com/2004_01_18_dneiwert_archive.html# 107466759817934752), and Tom Burka at American Street (www.reachm.com/amstreet/archives/000092.html).

Text of the 2004 State of the Union Address

◆━━◆━━◆━━◆━━◆

THE PRESIDENT: Mr. Speaker, Vice President Cheney, members of Congress, distinguished guests, and fellow citizens: America this evening is a nation called to great responsibilities. And we are rising to meet them.

As we gather tonight, hundreds of thousands of American servicemen and women are deployed across the world in the war on terror. By bringing hope to the oppressed, and delivering justice to the violent, they are making America more secure. (Applause.)

Each day, law enforcement personnel and intelligence officers are tracking terrorist threats; analysts are examining airline passenger lists; the men and women of our new Homeland Security Department are patrolling our coasts and borders. And their vigilance is protecting America. (Applause.)

VodkaPundit by Stephen Green, January 20, 2004
SOTU 07:12 PM

"They are making America more secure."

Bush leading off with a reminder about and a thank you to our troops in Iraq. Good applause, bipartisan even.

Followed by a thank you to airport screeners?

Spoken like a man who flies Air Force One.

Comments

► For all the complaints that TSA workers get, I've found them to be unfailingly polite and helpful the past few months, as we've been flying with two year old and an infant. They've gone above and beyond to help us through security without freaking out the kids. **Rabbi M. 07:44 PM**

Americans are proving once again to be the hardest working people in the world. The American economy is growing stronger. The tax relief you passed is working. (Applause.)

VodkaPundit by Stephen Green, January 20, 2004
SOTU 2 07:13 PM
"The tax relief you passed is working."
Left unsaid is the stimulus provided by reckless spending.

Tonight, members of Congress can take pride in the great works of compassion and reform that skeptics had thought impossible. You're raising the standards for our public schools, and you are giving our senior citizens prescription drug coverage under Medicare. (Applause.)

We have faced serious challenges together, and now we face a choice: We can go forward with confidence and resolve, or we can turn back to the dangerous illusion that terrorists are not plotting and outlaw regimes are no threat to us. We can press on with economic growth, and reforms in education and Medicare, or we can turn back to old policies and old divisions.

We've not come all this way—through tragedy, and trial and war—only to falter and leave our work unfinished. Americans are rising to the tasks of history, and they expect the same from us. In their efforts, their enterprise, and their character, the American people are showing that the state of our union is confident and strong. (Applause.)

VodkaPundit by Stephen Green, January 20, 2004
SOTU 3 07:14 PM
(Forgive typos in advance for the rest of the evening. We're playing fast and loose and fast.)
"The state of our Union is confident and strong."
Well, what did you expect him to say?
And with only a caveat or two, I'd have to agree.

Comments

· My caveats: Cut some social spending. Please, keep Greenspan from raising interest rates too early or fast. (Wait 'til summer and start .25 at a time.) Encourage higher education (not at universities, but trade schools and apprenticeships and mentorships). Don't mess with the constitution. Soon, we'll need to research stem cells (keep the brain-drain flowing). **aaron 07:36 PM**

VodkaPundit by Stephen Green, January 20, 2004
SOTU 4 07:15 PM
"We can press on..."
"We can continue..."
"...or leave our work unfinished."
Clearly this speech is, as everyone already knew, his first campaign commercial for 2004

Our greatest responsibility is the active defense of the American people. Twenty-eight months have passed since September 11th, 2001—over two years without an attack on American soil. And it is tempting to believe that the danger is behind us. That hope is understandable, comforting—and false. The killing has continued in Bali, Jakarta, Casablanca, Riyadh, Mombasa, Jerusalem, Istanbul, and Baghdad. The terrorists continue to plot against America and the civilized world. And by our will and courage, this danger will be defeated. (Applause.)

VodkaPundit by Stephen Green, January 20, 2004
SOTU 5 07:16 PM
"The terrorists continue to plot... and by our will, will be defeated."
That's exactly what I wanted to hear, but I'd rather get more specifics on how—some specific other than his current defense of the PATRIOT Act.

Inside the United States, where the war began, we must continue to give our homeland security and law enforcement personnel every tool they need to defend us. And one of those essential tools is the Patriot Act, which allows federal law enforcement to better share information, to track terrorists, to disrupt their cells, and to seize their assets. For years, we have used similar provisions to catch embezzlers and drug traffickers. If these methods are good for hunting criminals, they are even more important for hunting terrorists. (Applause.)

Key provisions of the Patriot Act are set to expire next year. (Applause.) The terrorist threat will not expire on that schedule. (Applause.) Our law enforcement needs this vital legislation to protect our citizens. You need to renew the Patriot Act. (Applause.)

VodkaPundit by Stephen Green, January 20, 2004
SOTU 6 07:17 PM

Ha! Weak applause from a certain side of the aisle when Bush commented that certain provisions of the PATRIOT Act are due to expire.

Pull the plug already.

Comments

► I think Bush set them up. I loved his line afterwards, and I'm not a big Patriot Act fan. **Cam 07:40 PM**

► Almost everything I've seen people scream about the Patriot Act in relation to has been FUD or misinformation. *Read the thing*, then draw conclusions. This one has been beaten to death. Here,[2] for example. **Mr. Lion 08:24 PM**

► Yup, this was a pre-planned sucker-punch that landed square on the donkey's chin. **Beldar 09:37 PM**

► Patriot Act. Benefit, modest. Costs, not significant. **aaron 09:49 PM**

► Stephen, Ask Nancy Pelosi about the Patriot Act. Even she admits she can't find on specific abuse of it. **Brian 11:49 PM**

► Get wise, Brian—sooner or later it'll be abused, and in such a way that you won't like it. What did Santayana say? **CTD on January 21, 2004 12:01 AM**

► "When they claim 10,000s of US citizens have been jailed due to the Act." I have never ever heard this and I read widely. Quit making s*** up. The very idea of the Patriot Act as a scared over-the-top response that leads to breaching many of the ideals that we hold as Americans. And no problem with you? Christ, I'm sad you're so scared. **Andrew I BYTE BACK[3] on January 21, 2004 01:25 AM**

► CTD, With all due respect sir, you get wise. Don't give me the usual "it violates civil liberties because it could be abused" slippery slope nonsense. You could say that about every law. I got arrested for vagrancy when I was 15!! for not having ID on me. Every law can be used nefariously. That's why we have juries. Even the ACLU and Dianne Feinstein (I said Pelosi before, but I was mistaken. They seem like the same woman half the time anyway) admits they can't find one real abuse of the act. You wise up and do some real research. Here's[4] a starting point: **Brian on January 22, 2004 01:50 AM**

America is on the offensive against the terrorists who started this war. Last March, Khalid Shaikh Mohammed, a mastermind of September the 11th, awoke to find himself in the custody of U.S. and Pakistani authorities. Last August the 11th brought the capture of the terrorist Hambali, who was a key player in the attack in Indonesia that killed over 200 people. We're tracking al Qaeda around the world, and nearly two-thirds of their known leaders have now been captured or killed. Thousands of very skilled and determined military personnel are on the manhunt, going after the remaining killers who hide in cities and caves, and one by one, we will bring these terrorists to justice. (Applause.)

> ### VodkaPundit by Stephen Green, January 20, 2004
> **SOTU 7 07:19 PM**
> "One by one, we will bring these terrorists to justice."
> "The US and our allies are determined: We refuse to live in the shadow of ultimate danger."
> Left unsaid was which allies. And that's fine, because hearing Germany, France, and Canada called "allies" is getting tiresome.

As part of the offensive against terror, we are also confronting the regimes that harbor and support terrorists, and could supply them with nuclear, chemical or biological weapons. The United States and our allies are determined: We refuse to live in the shadow of this ultimate danger. (Applause.)

The first to see our determination were the Taliban, who made Afghanistan the primary training base of al Qaeda killers. As of this month, that country has a new constitution, guaranteeing free elections and full participation by women. Businesses are opening, health care centers are being established, and the boys and girls of Afghanistan are back in school. With the help from the new Afghan army, our coalition is leading aggressive raids against the surviving members of the Taliban and al Qaeda. The men and women of Afghanistan are building a nation that is free and proud and fighting terror—and America is honored to be their friend. (Applause.)

Since we last met in this chamber, combat forces of the United States, Great Britain, Australia, Poland and other countries enforced the demands of the United Nations, ended the rule of Saddam Hussein, and the people of Iraq are free. (Applause.)

Having broken the Baathist regime, we face a remnant of violent Saddam supporters. Men who ran away from our troops in battle are now dispersed and attack from the shadows. These killers, joined by foreign terrorists, are a serious, continuing danger. Yet we're making progress against them. The once all-powerful ruler of Iraq was found in a hole, and now sits in a prison cell. (Applause.) Of the top 55 officials of the former regime, we have captured or killed 45. Our forces are on the offensive, leading over 1,600 patrols a day and conducting an average of 180 raids a week. We are dealing with these thugs in Iraq, just as surely as we dealt with Saddam Hussein's evil regime. (Applause.)

VodkaPundit by Stephen Green, January 20, 2004
SOTU 8 07:23 PM

"The people of Iraq are free."

Big applause from almost the entire chamber. Lord knows there are enough nutcases in Congress who still wonder if toppling Saddam was a "good thing."

I'd like to hear an admission that the administration underestimated postwar problems, but I doubt we'll get one.

Still—1,600 patrols a day, 18 raids a week sounds like pretty good work. And violence is down.

And he is still harping the end-of-June deadline for full Iraqi sovereignty

Bet that it will happen de jure—but not de facto.

The work of building a new Iraq is hard, and it is right. And America has always been willing to do what it takes for what is right. Last January, Iraq's only law was the whim of one brutal man. Today our coalition is working with the Iraqi Governing Council to draft a basic law, with a bill of rights. We're working with Iraqis and the United Nations to prepare for a transition to full Iraqi sovereignty by the end of June.

As democracy takes hold in Iraq, the enemies of freedom will do all in their power to spread violence and fear. They are trying to shake the will of our country and our friends, but the United States of America will never be intimidated by thugs and assassins. (Applause.) The killers will fail, and the Iraqi people will live in freedom. (Applause.)

Month by month, Iraqis are assuming more responsibility for their own security and their own future. And tonight we are honored to welcome one of Iraq's most respected leaders: the current President of the Iraqi Governing Council, Adnan Pachachi.

Sir, America stands with you and the Iraqi people as you build a free and peaceful nation. (Applause.)

VodkaPundit by Stephen Green, January 20, 2004
SOTU 9 07:25 PM
The IGC [Iraqi Governing Council] president—whose name I cannot type—is there.

It says something positive about our presence in his country that he isn't afraid to *leave* it. Saddam almost never left Iraq while he was in power. Dictators or weak leaders almost never do.

Comments
► Full-on war supporter here, but the IGC president isn't the leader of Iraq. Paul Bremer is—and he ain't weak. **MattJ 07:48 PM**

Because of American leadership and resolve, the world is changing for the better. Last month, the leader of Libya voluntarily pledged to disclose and dismantle all of his regime's weapons of mass destruction programs, including a uranium enrichment project for nuclear weapons. Colonel Qadhafi correctly judged that his country would be better off and far more secure without weapons of mass murder. (Applause.)

Nine months of intense negotiations involving the United States and Great Britain succeeded with Libya, while 12 years of diplomacy with Iraq did not. And one reason is clear: For diplomacy to be effective, words must be credible, and no one can now doubt the word of America. (Applause.)

Different threats require different strategies. Along with nations in the region, we're insisting that North Korea eliminate its nuclear program. America and the international community are demanding that Iran meet its commitments and not develop nuclear weapons. America is committed to keeping the world's most dangerous weapons out of the hands of the most dangerous regimes. (Applause.)

VodkaPundit by Stephen Green, January 20, 2004
SOTU 10 07:26 PM
Give the man his due—Bush is taking credit for Khaddy's sudden change of heart.

"Different threats require different strategies." So—on to North Korea...

Comments
► It just hit me who the 3 soldiers were...same ones that were on Time... **Mark 07:28 PM**

► Thanks for the tip! I missed that. **TM Lutas 09:24 PM**

When I came to this rostrum on September the 20th, 2001, I brought the police shield of a fallen officer, my reminder of lives that ended, and a task that does not end. I gave to you and to all Americans my complete commitment to securing our country and defeating our enemies. And this pledge, given by one, has been kept by many.

VodkaPundit by Stephen Green, January 20, 2004
SOTU 11 07:28 PM
Well. Almost nothing on North Korea.

Either something is brewing that can't be talked about, or nothing is going on at all.

(If it's the latter, don't fret. Doing nothing may be the best we can do for the time being with NK.)

Comments
► Something is always brewing, and because of the total unreliability of the other side (you can only count on bizarre abstinence, but not which issue you expect it to be about) there isn't anything to talk about. On a scale of clarity/ ambiguity, Iraq/North Korea are about at a 10/-1 for the famous Rumsfeld "Known knowns."[5] NK has been digging themselves into holes literally since the armistice in 1953 (which they do NOT consider to have been an end to the war) and they have made a very professional career out of creating "known unknowns." I.E; We think we know what we know, but we are very clear about the fact that what we think we know is very clearly in the "known unknowns" zone, because it is almost impossible to determine if our information is accurate. **Cletus on January 21, 2004 07:21 AM**

You in the Congress have provided the resources for our defense, and cast the difficult votes of war and peace. Our closest allies have been unwavering. America's intelligence personnel and diplomats have been skilled and tireless. And the men and women of the American military—they have taken the hardest duty. We've seen their skill and their courage in armored charges and midnight raids, and lonely hours on faithful watch. We have seen the joy when they return, and felt the sorrow when one is lost. I've had the honor of meeting our servicemen and women at many posts, from the deck of a carrier in the Pacific to a mess hall in Baghdad.

Many of our troops are listening tonight. And I want you and your families to know: America is proud of you. And my administration, and this Congress, will give you the resources you need to fight and win the war on terror. (Applause.)

VodkaPundit by Stephen Green, January 20, 2004
SOTU 12 07:29 PM

Bush thanked Congress for giving him the money to fight the war—and you better believed they enjoyed that stroke. Gave themselves a standing O (so to speak), they did.

Comments

► 536. Or a lot more if you count Cheney and the Cabinet. **charles austin 08:07 PM**

► House, Senate, Supreme Court Justices, Joint Chiefs, Cabinet, certain family members, the House is full for SOTU. There are a few exceptions. One member of the Cabinet and a member of Congress watch from bunkers. If the entire room is taken out, we have a President, a member of Congress, and can bootstrap back up from there. **TM Lutas 09:27 PM**

I know that some people question if America is really in a war at all. They view terrorism more as a crime, a problem to be solved mainly with law enforcement and indictments. After the World Trade Center was first attacked in 1993, some of the guilty were indicted and tried and convicted, and sent to prison. But the matter was not settled. The terrorists were still training and plotting in other nations, and drawing up more ambitious plans. After the chaos and carnage of September the 11th, it is not enough to serve our enemies with legal papers. The terrorists and their supporters declared war on the United States, and war is what they got. (Applause.)

Some in this chamber, and in our country, did not support the liberation of Iraq. Objections to war often come from principled motives. But let us be candid about the consequences of leaving Saddam Hussein in power. We're seeking all the facts. Already, the Kay Report identified dozens of weapons of mass destruction-related program activities[6] and significant amounts of equipment that Iraq concealed from the United Nations. Had we failed to act, the dictatator's weapons of mass destruction programs would continue to this day. Had we failed to act, Security Council resolutions on Iraq would have been revealed as empty threats, weakening the United Nations and encouraging defiance by dictators around the world. Iraq's torture chambers would still be filled with victims, terrified and innocent. The killing fields of Iraq—where hundreds of thousands of men and women and children vanished into the sands—would still be known only to the killers. For all who love freedom and peace, the world without Saddam Hussein's regime is a better and safer place. (Applause.)

> **Calpundit by Kevin Drum, January 20, 2004**
> 6:25—Did he really have the gall to pretend that the Kay report vindicated all the prewar WMD allegations?

> **VodkaPundit by Stephen Green, January 20, 2004**
> **SOTU 13 07:31 PM**
> Random thought: It's a bad sign for Bush, that a hawk like me is feeling secure enough to want him to finish up with the foreign policy already, and show me his domestic wares.
> If I'm that uninterested in foreign stuff already, then what's going through the head of more normal voters?
>
> **Comments**
> ► Really? I was eating it up. It was kind of like a rebuttal to twelve months of op/ed pieces. **Cam 07:39 PM**

Some critics have said our duties in Iraq must be internationalized. This particular criticism is hard to explain to our partners in Britain, Australia, Japan, South Korea, the Philippines, Thailand, Italy, Spain, Poland, Denmark, Hungary, Bulgaria, Ukraine, Romania, the Netherlands—(applause)—Norway, El Salvador, and the 17 other countries that have committed troops to Iraq. (Applause.) As we debate at home, we must never ignore the vital contributions of our international partners, or dismiss their sacrifices.

From the beginning, America has sought international support for our operations in Afghanistan and Iraq, and we have gained much support. There is a difference, however, between leading a coalition of many nations, and submitting to the objections of a few. America will never seek a permission slip to defend the security of our country. (Applause.)

VodkaPundit by Stephen Green, January 20, 2004
SOTU 14 07:33 PM

Take THAT, vile French b******s! (I mean you, too, John Kerry.)

Bush just listed (all but 17!) our international allies, and he went on longer than Howard Dean shouting out the states where he had not yet begun to fight.

So... uh... take that, vile French bastards.

I feel better now.

Comments

► "That line of criticism is a little hard to explain to our allies in Britain, Australia..." Line of the night, IMHO.[7] **John Cole 07:40 PM**

► YAAAARRRRHHHHHHH! **Jediflyer 07:58 PM**

► Jeez, how much more unilateral can you get when Mongolia and Japan are doing their part? so the franco-sphere stayed home this time, so what. **Frank Martin 08:11 PM**

► Why don't people open their mind a little and consider that this speaks so much more about France and Russia than US. **aaron 08:55 PM**

► SG, You failed to hear Pretty-girl Nancy, who said "true" international allies. The Liberal-Hypocrites do not consider Poland (e.g.) as a true international ally. The only true allies are French and Germans. PS: I do not eat french food or drink french vine. I do not care much of Oktoberfest. I am an American—so sue me. **AKB Ali Karim Bey 09:29 PM**

► France is a tourist attraction. Nothing else without what we built. **aaron 09:46 PM**

► I don't quite understand the contempt for France and Germany alongside the admiration for democracy and freedom. France and Germany are democracies and the people are free. I thought that was what we admired. Or is the thought that "true" democracies always agree with the US (or at least the Republican party)? **BayMike 09:48 PM**

► It's a reaction to their contempt, not lack of agreement. **aaron 10:11 PM**

► Don't have much of a problem with Germany. I think they're just a little naive. **aaron 10:13 PM**

► "France is a tourist attraction. Nothing else without what we built". Aaron, allow me a troll moment, but this strikes me as utterly stupid. "We" didn't build jack but Eurodisney. And you had a point ???? Non? **Andrew I BYTE BACK January 21, 2004 01:20 AM**

► Andrew, I guess you've never heard of the Marshall Plan, without which Western Europe would not have recovered from WWII until the mid-1960s. BayMike: As to Germany and their role in the Axis of Weasels, it is primarily due to their current leadership. (Remember that the governing coalition includes the Green Party.) Angela Merkel, leader of the CDU (the opposition, and possibly the next chancellor of Germany) was a vocal supporter of the war effort. While the CDU was divided by the issue, most of the leaders sup-ported Merkel. France, on the other hand, didn't even take a principled stand against us; they flat-out stated that they would veto any UNSC resolution that authorized force, regardless of the circumstances. That is not the attitude of an ally. They may be democratic, but that attitude is blatantly anti-American. **timekeeper on January 21, 2004 03:39 AM**

► John Kerry was on the news repeating the same thing as these aren't real allies. What a moron. **Kevin on January 21, 2004 07:05 AM**

► Hmmm, when was the last time France won a war (either one they started, or otherwise)? I think of Napoleon (whose reach exceeded his grasp), and after that, all I can think of is the Franco-Prussian War (Alsace captured by the Germans), World War I (hmmm, US saved France's butts), World War II (ditto, in spades; France actually SURRENDERED again). After that, the Empire began to crumble, with French colonies in the Middle East, Africa, and Indochina revolting against the colonial masters. (The same can be said of all the European colonial powers; some simply held on longer than others.) Today, the glorious French empire stretches from Nice to Brest, with Martinique, Guadeloupe, St. Pierre and Miquelon, and a few lumps of Pacific coral thrown in for good measure. **timekeeper on January 21, 2004 10:00 AM**

We also hear doubts that democracy is a realistic goal for the greater Middle East, where freedom is rare. Yet it is mistaken, and condescending, to assume that whole cultures and great religions are incompatible with liberty and self-government. I believe that God has planted in every human heart the desire to live in freedom. And even when that desire is crushed by tyranny for decades, it will rise again. (Applause.)

VodkaPundit by Stephen Green, January 20, 2004
SOTU 15 07:35 PM

'It is mistaken and condescending..."

...to think that some cultures or religions are incompatible with liberty.

It's a great line, my favorite so far, and he's using it to sell a doubling of some propaganda program?

Now you know, in a nutshell, what I find so wonderful/ reprehensible about this President.

Comments

► Yep, love him and hate him. Unfortunately, as for his Democratic opponents, it's mostly hate (ok, a very strong dislike and disdain, not hate). Sometimes it sucks to be a small government libertarian. **Russ Goble 08:36 PM**

As long as the Middle East remains a place of tyranny and despair and anger, it will continue to produce men and movements that threaten the safety of America and our friends. So America is pursuing a forward strategy of freedom in the greater Middle East. We will challenge the enemies of reform, confront the allies of terror, and expect a higher standard from our friend. To cut through the barriers of hateful propaganda, the Voice of America and other broadcast services are expanding their programming in Arabic and Persian—and soon, a new television service will begin providing reliable news and information across the region. I will send you a proposal to double the budget of the

National Endowment for Democracy, and to focus its new work on the development of free elections, and free markets, free press, and free labor unions in the Middle East. And above all, we will finish the historic work of democracy in Afghanistan and Iraq, so those nations can light the way for others, and help transform a troubled part of the world. (Applause.)

Calpundit by Kevin Drum, January 20, 2004

6:35—So far the entire SOTU has just been platitudes about Iraq and the war on terror. That's fine, but when do we get something concrete?

America is a nation with a mission, and that mission comes from our most basic beliefs. We have no desire to dominate, no ambitions of empire. Our aim is a democratic peace—a peace founded upon the dignity and rights of every man and woman. America acts in this cause with friends and allies at our side, yet we understand our special calling: This great republic will lead the cause of freedom. (Applause.)

In the last three years, adversity has also revealed the fundamental strengths of the American economy. We have come through recession, and terrorist attack, and corporate scandals, and the uncertainties of war. And because you acted to stimulate our economy with tax relief, this economy is strong, and growing stronger. (Applause.)

VodkaPundit by Stephen Green, January 20, 2004

SOTU 16 07:38 PM

"We've come through recession, terrorist attack, corporate scandals, and the uncertainty of war...

...and this economy is strong and growing stronger"
And he's thanking his tax cuts for it.

He's got a good case, but he's mostly playing defense on the economy. If he doesn't change his tune (or at least his tempo) the Democrats will eat him alive on this one.

Comments

► How is he playing defense? We have low interest rates, a growing economy (8.2% in the 3rd quarter), a Dow over 10,000, NASDAQ over 2,000 (both two year highs) and recent jobs growth (unemployment is 5.7% and declining). Federal spending is out of control yes, but deficits during

> recessions are prudent. I'd like to see Federal spending
> contract and the deficit decline. Unfortunately, deficit
> hawks rarely win elections. **Gary B 08:04 PM**

You have doubled the child tax credit from $500 to $1,000, reduced the marriage penalty, begun to phase out the death tax, reduced taxes on capital gains and stock dividends, cut taxes on small businesses, and you have lowered taxes for every American who pays income taxes.

Americans took those dollars and put them to work, driving this economy forward. The pace of economic growth in the third quarter of 2003 was the fastest in nearly 20 years; new home construction, the highest in almost 20 years; home ownership rates, the highest ever. Manufacturing activity is increasing. Inflation is low. Interest rates are low. Exports are growing. Productivity is high, and jobs are on the rise. (Applause.)

These numbers confirm that the American people are using their money far better than government would have—and you were right to return it. (Applause.)

> **Calpundit by Kevin Drum, January 20, 2004**
> **6:40**—The people are spending their tax money better than
> the government could have? But isn't the government still
> spending all that money too?

America's growing economy is also a changing economy. As technology transforms the way almost every job is done, America becomes more productive, and workers need new skills. Much of our job growth will be found in high-skilled fields like health care and biotechnology. So we must respond by helping more Americans gain the skills to find good jobs in our new economy.

> **VodkaPundit by Stephen Green, January 20, 2004**
> **SOTU 17 07:39 PM**
> "Much of our job growth will be in high-tech fields..."
> Which, sigh, leads to Bush selling high tech jobs training.
> Maybe I liked it better when he was still talking war, after all.

Comments

► "Much of our job growth will be in high-tech fields . . ." that will promptly get shipped to India and Pakistan!!! (Standing ovation from Fortune 100 I.T. departments). Gimme more info on that, Georgie, or I remain unimpressed. **jason 09:14 PM**

All skills begin with the basics of reading and math, which are supposed to be learned in the early grades of our schools. Yet for too long, for too many children, those skills were never mastered. By passing the No Child Left Behind Act, you have made the expectation of literacy the law of our country. We're providing more funding for our schools—a 36-percent increase since 2001. We're requiring higher standards. We are regularly testing every child on the fundamentals. We are reporting results to parents, and making sure they have better options when schools are not performing. We are making progress toward excellence for every child in America. (Applause.)

VodkaPundit by Stephen Green, January 20, 2004
SOTU 18 07:42 PM
I can see it already: No Child Left Behind will (along with that pricey Medicare reform law) be the centerpiece of his reelection campaign.
Ugh.

Comments

► Portable health insurance via HSAs isn't bad. It cuts your dependence on employers and is probably the brightest part of the medicare bill. I also like the tort reform bits. **TM Lutas 09:32 PM**

► I'm not crazy about NCLB but the soccer mom's wanted big brother to do something about education and he's doing it. You may not like the result but it's not just the lip service the donk's give us. **roux on January 21, 2004 08:12 AM**

But the status quo always has defenders. Some want to undermine the No Child Left Behind Act by weakening standards and accountability. Yet the results we require are really a matter of common sense: We expect third graders to read and do math at the third grade level—and that's not asking too much. Testing is the only way to identify and help students who are falling behind. This nation will not go back to the days of simply shuffling children along from grade to grade without them learning the basics. I refuse to give up on any child—and the No Child Left Behind Act is opening the door of opportunity to all of America's children. (Applause.)

At the same time, we must ensure that older students and adults can gain the skills they need to find work now. Many of the fastest growing occupations require strong math and science preparation, and training beyond the high school level. So tonight, I propose a series of measures called Jobs for the 21st Century. This program will provide extra help to middle and high school students who fall behind in reading and math, expand advanced placement programs in low-income schools, invite math and science professionals from the private sector to teach part-time in our high schools. I propose larger Pell grants for students who prepare for college with demanding courses in high school. (Applause.) I propose increasing our support for America's fine community colleges, so they can—(applause.) I do so, so they can train workers for industries that are creating the most new jobs. By all these actions, we'll help more and more Americans to join in the growing prosperity of our country. Job training is important, and so is job creation.

> ### Calpundit by Kevin Drum, January 20, 2004
> **6:44**—A standing O for increased support for community colleges?

We must continue to pursue an aggressive, pro-growth economic agenda. (Applause.) Congress has some unfinished business on the issue of taxes. The tax reductions you passed are set to expire. Unless you act—(applause)—unless you act—unless you act, the unfair tax on marriage will go back up. Unless you act, millions of families will be charged $300 more in federal taxes for every child. Unless you act, small businesses will pay higher taxes. Unless you act, the death tax will eventually come back to life. Unless you act, Americans face a tax increase. What Congress has given, the Congress should not take away. For the sake of job growth, the tax cuts you passed should be permanent. (Applause.)

VodkaPundit by Stephen Green, January 20, 2004
SOTU 19 07:44 PM
"We must continue to pursue an aggressive, pro-growth economic agenda..."
And how? He wants his tax cuts permanent. This stuff is going to sail through the House, but the Senate is going to require some serious horse trading.
Already, Democrats are booing him (real boos there in the chamber), Republicans are going nuts.
It'll be on the front burner for spring and summer, and is politically very, very smart. More on this one later, if I remember.
Someone wanna remind me?

Comments
► Stephen, Don't forget to talk about the stuff about that thing... **Greg 10:44 PM**

Our agenda for jobs and growth must help small business owners and employees with relief from needless federal regulation, and protect them from junk and frivolous lawsuits. (Applause.)

Consumers and businesses need reliable supplies of energy to make our economy run—so I urge you to pass legislation to modernize our electricity system, promote conservation, and make America less dependent on foreign sources of energy. (Applause.)

Calpundit by Kevin Drum, January 20, 2004
6:45—Lots of good words about energy policy. Too bad none of that stuff is actually in the energy bill he's trying to get through Congress.

My administration is promoting free and fair trade to open up new markets for America's entrepreneurs and manufacturers and farmers—to create jobs for American workers. Younger workers should have the opportunity to build a nest egg by saving part of their Social Security taxes in a personal retirement account. (Applause.) We should make the Social Security system a source of ownership for the American people. (Applause.) And we should limit the burden of government on this economy by acting as good stewards of taxpayers' dollars. (Applause.)

VodkaPundit by Stephen Green, January 20, 2004
SOTU 20 07:45 PM

"My administration is promoting free *and fair* trade..." (Emphasis added.)

With Dick Gephardt gone, I'd have thought the last Fair Trader had left the building. Shoulda known better.

Comments

► Which probably means "fair trade" is part of the lexicon now. Not good. **Russ Goble 08:39 PM**

In two weeks, I will send you a budget that funds the war, protects the homeland, and meets important domestic needs, while limiting the growth in discretionary spending to less than four percent. (Applause.) This will require that Congress focus on priorities, cut wasteful spending, and be wise with the people's money. By doing so, we can cut the deficit in half over the next five years. (Applause.)

Calpundit by Kevin Drum, January 20, 2004
6:48—We can cut the deficit in half in five years, apparently by limiting the growth in discretionary spending to 4%? This simply defies all reason. That won't even come close to cutting the deficit in half.

VodkaPundit by Stephen Green, January 20, 2004
SOTU 21 07:47 PM

"...limiting the growth in discretionary spending to no more than 2%"

How about a real CUT, goddamnit? We've seen double-digit growth three years running. Just cutting the rate of growth just doesn't cut it.

Comments

► I heard 4%. **Spoons 07:51 PM**

► Spoons is right, but he said under 4%. It's likely to be 3.99% **Gary B 07:55 PM**

► I'm almost positive he promised a 4% growth rate in discretionary spending LAST YEAR. Which tells you how well he'll stick to THAT number. **Russ Goble 08:41 PM**

► He said no more than 4% increase in discretionary spending. Left unsaid was how much the rest of the spending was increasing, and what the overall increase would be. It makes me skeptical of any plan to reduce the deficit. **Shawn Levasseur 08:57 PM**

► I expect that better margins in the Congress will reduce the need for the horse trading that is ballooning expenditures. If 2005 rolls around and things are not greatly improved on spending 2006 is going to be a very good year for Democrats. **TM Lutas 09:35 PM**

Tonight, I also ask you to reform our immigration laws so they reflect our values and benefit our economy. I propose a new temporary worker program to match willing foreign workers with willing employers when no Americans can be found to fill the job. This reform will be good for our economy because employers will find needed workers in an honest and orderly system. A temporary worker program will help protect our homeland, allowing Border Patrol and law enforcement to focus on true threats to our national security.

I oppose amnesty, because it would encourage further illegal immigration, and unfairly reward those who break our laws. My temporary worker program will preserve the citizenship path for those who respect the law, while bringing millions of hardworking men and women out from the shadows of American life. (Applause.)

VodkaPundit by Stephen Green, January 20, 2004
SOTU 22 07:48 PM
Now, selling his immigration reform plan.
   For, I think the first time, Bush used the word "amnesty."
   Conservative hair just stood on end all over the nation.
That's not playing to his base, that's peeing on the electric fence.
   NOTE: His plan strikes me as a worthy moral and political goal, but too intrusive to work as advertised.

Comments

► It's the first time I heard the word "amnesty" too...but he coupled it with two other very important words: "I OPPOSE..." Outstanding! **Offutt_Major 07:51 PM**

► I was going to say exactly what Offutt Major said. **Cam 07:52 PM**

► Are you even listening?!? He said NO amnesty (like above comments). And he talked about owners and players taking care of steroids, not the feds. You need the wax cleaned out of your ears. **Director Mitch 08:11 PM**

Our nation's health care system, like our economy, is also in a time of change. Amazing medical technologies are improving and saving lives. This dramatic progress has brought its own challenge, in the rising costs of medical care and health insurance. Members of Congress, we must work together to help control those costs and extend the benefits of modern medicine throughout our country. (Applause.)

Meeting these goals requires bipartisan effort, and two months ago, you showed the way. By strengthening Medicare and adding a prescription drug benefit, you kept a basic commitment to our seniors: You are giving them the modern medicine they deserve. (Applause.)

Starting this year, under the law you passed, seniors can choose to receive a drug discount card, saving them 10 to 25 percent off the retail price of most prescription drugs—and millions of low-income seniors can get an additional $600 to buy medicine. Beginning next year, seniors will have new coverage for preventive screenings against diabetes and heart disease, and seniors just entering Medicare can receive wellness exams.

In January of 2006, seniors can get prescription drug coverage under Medicare. For a monthly premium of about $35, most seniors who do not have that coverage today can expect to see their drug bills cut roughly in half. Under this reform, senior citizens will be able to keep their Medicare just as it is, or they can choose a Medicare plan that fits them best—just as you, as members of Congress, can choose an insurance plan that meets your needs. And starting this year, millions of Americans will be able to save money tax-free for their medical expenses in a health savings account. (Applause.)

VodkaPundit by Stephen Green, January 20, 2004
SOTU 23 07:50 PM
Yawn. Medicare reform.
To paraphrase:
"Money! I'm giving you money! I'm saving you money!"
To Bush's credit, he said it a little more artfully.

Comments

► You and I have the same reaction to Medicare talk. It just puts me to sleep. **Cam 07:51 PM**

► The technology infrastructure stuff is pretty good from an efficiency standpoint. You wouldn't believe how much money goes down a rathole with insurance forms and approvals. **TM Lutas 09:37 PM**

I signed this measure proudly, and any attempt to limit the choices of our seniors, or to take away their prescription drug coverage under Medicare, will meet my veto. (Applause.)

Calpundit by Kevin Drum, January 20, 2004

6:51—Any attempt to take away Medicare prescription benefits will "meet...my...veto." Huh? Who's proposing that? Especially given that Republicans control both houses of Congress?

Comments

► The Repubs are risking injuries to their hamstrings with all the ups and downs. Did Rove install seat buzzers for them? **lk 6:51 PM**

VodkaPundit by Stephen Green, January 20, 2004

SOTU 24 07:51 PM

So NOW he threatens a veto? Over Medical Savings Accounts?
Weak.

Comments

► Is it me, or does Senator Ted look like he's passing a stone? **Frank Martin 07:54 PM**

► I think the threatened Veto was if congress ever moved to take away the new medicare benefits recently passed. Fat chance of that happening, if anything the Dems would increase such benefits. **Shawn Levasseur 09:05 PM**

► Health Savings Accounts (HSAs) are going to be "very" important in labor relations. A lot of people are sticking around for health benefits. If they can build their own plans and save a load of money by adopting better lifestyle and healthcare spending practices, this is going to really change the US. **TM Lutas 09:39 PM**

► Medical savings account benefit is a very good concept. It should ease the burden on the younger generations and generations into the future. How early can you start one? Setting aside money for private health care instead of state provided sounds good to me. Putting the money aside by choice will also show the demand and who it comes from, helping the health care industry identify areas for growth.
aaron on January 21, 2004 09:00 AM

On the critical issue of health care, our goal is to ensure that Americans can choose and afford private health care coverage that best fits their individual needs. To make insurance more affordable, Congress must act to address rapidly rising health care costs. Small businesses should be able to band together and negotiate for lower insurance rates, so they can cover more workers with health insurance. I urge you to pass association health plans. (Applause.) I ask you to give lower-income Americans a refundable tax credit that would allow millions to buy their own basic health insurance. (Applause.)

By computerizing health records, we can avoid dangerous medical mistakes, reduce costs, and improve care. To protect the doctor-patient relationship, and keep good doctors doing good work, we must eliminate wasteful and frivolous medical lawsuits. (Applause.) And tonight I propose that individuals who buy catastrophic health care coverage, as part of our new health savings accounts, be allowed to deduct 100 percent of the premiums from their taxes. (Applause.)

Calpundit by Kevin Drum, January 20, 2004
6:54—This is the second time he's talked about eliminating frivolous lawsuits. But what's his proposal for doing this?

VodkaPundit by Stephen Green, January 20, 2004
SOTU 25 07:53
I'm right now watching Hillary Clinton applaud tort reform for medical lawsuits.

Either she's really moving to the center—which would explain the lack of lightning bolts, earth not opening to swallow her whole, etc.—or god doesn't watch the news.

On a similar note, they caught Charles Rangel napping.

Comments
- ► She did not look like she was sincere in her applause, more like she thought he was funny. **aaron 07:55 PM**
- ► I noticed the same thing. Weird. Ted Kennedy doesn't seem to be enjoying himself, does he? **Fredrik Nyman 07:58 PM**
- ► Ted Kennedy was certainly not enjoying himself at all. We were taking bets on which of the arteries in his brain was going to let go first. **tbrosz 08:49 PM**
- ► I think she is trying to move to the center. Remember when she was in Iraq at the same time as Bush? She was busily applauding the "mission" (although, from the frozen smiles on the troops around her, I think they bought it about as much as I did). **cerberus 09:57 PM**

VodkaPundit by Stephen Green, January 20, 2004
SOTU 26 07:54 PM
Just got an email telling me I typo'ed—Bush wants a 4% limit in spending growth, not 2% as I said earlier.

Comments
- ► oops... sorry for piling on in the comments of the earlier post, as I had yet to read this one.... **Shawn Levasseur 09:07 PM**

A government-run health care system is the wrong prescription. (Applause.) By keeping costs under control, expanding access, and helping more Americans afford coverage, we will preserve the system of private medicine that makes America's health care the best in the world. (Applause.)

Calpundit by Kevin Drum, January 20, 2004
6:55—Lots of retrospective stuff so far: the war was great, the Medicare bill was great, NCLB was great, etc. etc. But really, not much in the way of new policy proposals.

We are living in a time of great change—in our world, in our economy, in science and medicine. Yet some things endure—courage and compassion, reverence and integrity, respect for differences of faith and race. The values we try to live by never change. And they are instilled in us by fundamental institutions, such as families and schools and religious congregations. These institutions, these unseen pillars of civilization, must remain strong in America, and we will defend them.

We must stand with our families to help them raise healthy, responsible children. When it comes to helping children make right choices, there is work for all of us to do.

One of the worst decisions our children can make is to gamble their lives and futures on drugs. Our government is helping parents confront this problem with aggressive education, treatment, and law enforcement. Drug use in high school has declined by 11 percent over the last two years. Four hundred thousand fewer young people are using illegal drugs than in the year 2001. (Applause.) In my budget, I proposed new funding to continue our aggressive, community-based strategy to reduce demand for illegal drugs. Drug testing in our schools has proven to be an effective part of this effort. So tonight I proposed an additional $23 million for schools that want to use drug testing as a tool to save children's lives. The aim here is not to punish children, but to send them this message: We love you, and we don't want to lose you. (Applause.)

VodkaPundit by Stephen Green, January 20, 2004
SOTU 27 07:55 PM
More money for school drug testing, because "we love you."
   You know, I wish I'd heard that line when I was still single. In the bars, "Grab your ankles; I love you" might have worked wonders.

Comments
- ► That's horrible. Really, I know a lot of good people who wouldn't have made it far in life without some drugs. **aaron 08:00 PM**
- ► For example, President George W. Bush. **Megan 08:18 PM**
- ► Actually, most people I know. **aaron 08:52 PM**
- ► I call dibs on the entire "SOTU 27" post as an email sig. **Reginleif the Valkyrie 09:03 PM**
- ► "We're tossing you in jail for decades, because we love you" Teaching a new generation to learn to live without civil rights.... Thank god for rebellious teenagers. (Why no, I'm not a parent... why do you ask?). **Shawn Levasseur 09:09 PM**
- ► It works at my bar! **Sean Kirby 09:34 PM**
- ► I blogged on this one already. This is a winner for the anti-drug warriors but you have to embrace the love bit, not make fun of it.

> We can't show our love for them if we expose the drug test results to the cops and they're off to jail, now can we? Love your children, love your neighbor, it doesn't work well with a criminal justice model. GWB opened the door a crack to a good place. **TM Lutas 09:42 PM**

To help children make right choices, they need good examples. Athletics play such an important role in our society, but, unfortunately, some in professional sports are not setting much of an example. The use of performance-enhancing drugs like steroids in baseball, football, and other sports is dangerous, and it sends the wrong message—that there are shortcuts to accomplishment, and that performance is more important than character. So tonight I call on team owners, union representatives, coaches, and players to take the lead, to send the right signal, to get tough, and to get rid of steroids now. (Applause.)

Calpundit by Kevin Drum, January 20, 2004
6:57—Get rid of steroids in professional sports? What the heck is that doing in the SOTU?

VodkaPundit by Stephen Green, January 20, 2004
SOTU 28 07:56 PM
Federal action against STEROIDS?
   On domestic policy, Bush is the Republican Bill Clinton. No issue is too small to get his attention, if he can throw a few million dollars at it and claim "progress."

Comments
- ► Wasted airtime IMO...beneath SOTU. **Offutt_Major 07:57 PM**
- ► He called on team owners, etc. He said not a word about fed $. This is called standing on top of the soap box. Wait for reaction from said team owners, etc. I think you got a little carried away. Spouse and I sorta did a "huh, that's not exactly SOTU topic-worthy," but didn't get into a huff. **Director Mitch 08:09 PM**
- ► Go Pats. Go Tom Brady. I have no problem with President telling rich athletes to set a good example. **rrsafety 08:32 PM**
- ► It's called the bully pulpit. I actually don't have a problem with him saying what he said about steroids. It's kind of

refreshing having something in the SOTU not have a price tag attached to it. But, I agree that it seems out of place and kind of out of left field (hmmm....where Barry Bonds plays...hmmm) in the context of the overall speech. Not sure what he was trying to accomplish. Seems like a better place for it would have been while meeting the Super Bowl winner at the White House in a month or so. **Russ Goble 08:49 PM**

► GWB is just bitter about Roger Maris losing his record. . .:-) **M. Scott Eiland 09:07 PM**

► Note that the WNBA and the NFL were represented, but I saw no representative of major league baseball in the audience. I'll be tuning into the late SportsCenter on ESPN... It should be interesting to see if they cover the sports angle of the SOTU. If they are on the ball they will have a story. (Nothing on ESPN.com yet) **Shawn Levasseur 09:14 PM**

► This was moral suasion from a former major-league team co-owner to his former colleagues. If they don't respond, immediately and bigtime, they'll be shamed. Not a single taxpayer dollar involved—rather, a hugely cost-effective use of the bully pulpit. **Beldar 09:34 PM**

► I agree that it was a great bully pulpit moment. It was also probably the most pro-libertarian anti-drug message at least since Nancy Reagan. **TM Lutas 09:45 PM**

To encourage right choices, we must be willing to confront the dangers young people face—even when they're difficult to talk about. Each year, about 3 million teenagers contract sexually-transmitted diseases that can harm them, or kill them, or prevent them from ever becoming parents. In my budget, I propose a grassroots campaign to help inform families about these medical risks. We will double federal funding for abstinence programs, so schools can teach this fact of life: Abstinence for young people is the only certain way to avoid sexually-transmitted diseases. (Applause.)

Decisions children now make can affect their health and character for the rest of their lives. All of us—parents and schools and government—must work together to counter the negative influence of the culture, and to send the right messages to our children.

VodkaPundit by Stephen Green, January 20, 2004
SOTU 29 07:58 PM
Schools, parents, AND government must fight popular culture's influence on children?
One outta three, Mr. President—that's pretty bad.

Comments
► Remember the "Moral Majority" movements in the early/ mid '80's??? THAT'S more like what that section sounded like..... **Jim S on January 21, 2004 11:03 AM**

A strong America must also value the institution of marriage. I believe we should respect individuals as we take a principled stand for one of the most fundamental, enduring institutions of our civilization. Congress has already taken a stand on this issue by passing the Defense of Marriage Act, signed in 1996 by President Clinton. That statute protects marriage under federal law as a union of a man and a woman, and declares that one state may not redefine marriage for other states.

Activist judges, however, have begun redefining marriage by court order, without regard for the will of the people and their elected representatives. On an issue of such great consequence, the people's voice must be heard. If judges insist on forcing their arbitrary will upon the people, the only alternative left to the people would be the constitutional process. Our nation must defend the sanctity of marriage. (Applause.)

The outcome of this debate is important—and so is the way we conduct it. The same moral tradition that defines marriage also teaches that each individual has dignity and value in God's sight. (Applause.)

Calpundit by Kevin Drum, January 20, 2004
6:59—So does he want a marriage amendment or not? It would be nice if he'd give us a straight answer on this one of these days.

VodkaPundit by Stephen Green, January 20, 2004
SOTU 30 08:00 PM
"If judges insist on enforcing their arbitrary will on the people..."
Bush just caved in to those who would amend the Constitution to forbid gay marriage.

I'll be checking in later with Andrew Sullivan[8] for a reply more coherent (and more personal) than anything I could write right now.

Comments

► Step back from this one. Its a hidden two-edged sword. He is in there, to many, because of a court. Fighting the current overstepping of the Judicial Branch is something he has to do quietly. Don't say anything publically. Make Congress do the dirty work. **Niall G. 08:08 PM**

► Here, I think he's just words. I don't think he'll act, and if he does it will piss people off, but not affect much. Plus, any damage he might do (which I strongly doubt) won't be too costly and can be reversed as easily as enacted. **aaron 08:11 PM**

► Have to check, but don't believe he actually said he backs the marriage amendment. He just said the people should be allowed to choose. Sounded to me more like a CYA for the conservative base, without actually saying he backs the amendment. **Jim 08:12 PM**

► Step back and think a bit on this one. The issue is not about gay marriage as much as it is about judicial tyranny. It would be obtuse to suggest gay marriage isn't a significant part of it, but, the key issue is something else, and a lot of people are blinded by the former. **Mr. Lion 08:19 PM**

► Regardless of the legal reality, he just used the bully pulpit to paint my relationship as a threat to America. **Michael 08:33 PM**

► The beauty of the United States is that the people of Vermont can offer same sex civil unions while the people of Tennessee can "protect" the institution of marriage by maintaining the status quo. There is room in this amazing republic for all views to be protected almost simultaneously. **Megan 08:42 PM**

► Michael, I hope not (I wasn't listening well).

He didn't say anything about gay marriage. He supported hetero marriage. That is in national interest.

Gay marriage, while I support morally, may open the door for abuse (by heteros). I believe instead that there should be a separate civil union for gays, and marriage for gays when adoption is involved. **aaron 08:44 PM**

► "And there's no need for passing such an amendment anyway. The Tenth Amendment already guarantees the states the right to define marriage any way they want."

Unless, of course, a left-of-center judge decides to say otherwise when DOMA is challenged, and the appellate courts decide not to disagree. Plessy v. Ferguson and "separate but equal" were the black letter law of the land in 1952—things changed rather abruptly. It's one thing to think that opponents of gay marriage are misguided, or even outright bigoted. It's quite another to say that they don't have historical reasons for thinking that the federal courts are a threat to their POV. **M. Scott Eiland 09:05 PM**

► He might be trying to keep another issue like abortion to crop up. Not remembering the time period I have read there was an evolution going on abortion in America. Maybe in another five years (I'm guessing) the US would have reached a consensus on abortion and a lot of heartache and trouble would have been avoided. Instead the Supreme Court imposed by fiat a set of conditions and in response people hardened their positions.

If we let the citizens come to a position on their own, then we will have less trouble in the long run. The road may appear to be longer but less rocky. **Richard Swan 09:09 PM**

► Sound and Fury topic to mollify the social conservatives. **Shawn Levasseur 09:16 PM**

► Game theory: Right now, it is not in the interest of the state (re nation) to prohibit abortion. I can only think of two reasons it would. One, risk of invasion. Two, we don't have an acceptable supply of immigrants. This makes it unlikely that it would ever be in interest of the state to prohibit abortion.

Ironically, if people exercise their abortion option too often, anti-abortionist should eventually outnumber the pro-choicers/planned parents. **aaron 09:33 PM**

► The beauty of the American system is that it strikes a very neat balance between institutional inertia and popular opinion, while retaining flexibility in moving the center of gravity.

Take, for instance, the notion of obscenity. Back when I was a kid, the stuff currently on prime-time TV could have resulted in jail time even if shown in private clubs or residences. Yet, today, with many of the same laws still on the books, it is recognized that incarceration should be reserved for those who seriously harm the body politic—and not those who merely titillate.

Much as I appreciate Sullivan's blog, and supportive as I am toward those whose love rides in the back of the bus of current law, the pragmatic view is that the struggle is in hearts, not in law.

I truly believe that "Queer Eye" on national TV has done more good than "Defense of Marriage" on the statute books has done harm. If most of the US is convinced that love is love, intimate personal relationships are the basis of community, that "all the world loves a lover," and that societal support for long-term, stable, forward-looking pair bonds (Britney notwithstanding) promotes the common good—well, then, it won't much matter what statutes were enacted in prior years.

The US system can bend without breaking. Laws can be repealed, enforcement can be "de-prioritized," judgments can be overturned. Once the center of gravity shifts, it doesn't much matter what goes on at the fringes. The trick is to make that shift. **cthulhu 09:54 PM**

► "If judges insist on enforcing their arbitrary will on the people..."

Bush could have stopped right there, and not even mentioned gay marriage, or mentioned it and a host of other things. That is the crux of why I am against gay marriage: I am tired of having the laws imposed on me by liberal judges like that ACLU hack Steven Reinhardt. And, I am tired of being called a bigot because I don't parrot the militant gay agenda. Look, who you love is your business. Whether I think your relationship should be given the same rights as a heterosexual one is mine. Think about how far the gay cause has come: From the closet, to tolerance of it, to acceptance of it, to celebration of it. I think it is most appropriate to draw the line at marriage.

Mr. Green has said that he is a "first amendment absolutist." He'd agree that my view should be heard, whether he agrees or not. If you want to say I am a homophobe (I don't know how, I have no fear of men) or a bigot, then OK. I agree with Mr. Green's First Amendment views. **Brian 11:42 PM**

► One more thing: M. Scott Eiland said:

> "And there's no need for passing such an amendment anyway. The Tenth Amendment already guarantees the states the right to define marriage any way they want.
>
> "Unless, of course, a left-of-center judge decides to say otherwise when DOMA is challenged, and the appellate courts decide not to disagree. Plessy v. Ferguson and 'separate but equal' were the black letter law of the land in 1952—things changed rather abruptly. It's one thing to think that opponents of gay marriage are misguided, or even outright bigoted. It's quite another to say that they don't have historical reasons for thinking that the federal courts are a threat to their POV."

I'll answer like this: The liberal judges will run to the "full faith and credit clause" to impose their will on every state to accept a marriage under Vermont (or Hawaii, or any state) law. And, Plessy is a FALSE analogy. Rights based on who you go to bed with are not the same as the color of your skin. I am severely tired of hearing that comparison. **Brian 11:46 PM**

► If the majority are in favor of gay marriage, then let each state have a referendum, to settle it once an for all. I'll support it fully (even after I vote against it) if the majority of my State votes for it. Simple as that. I don't want judicial imposed law. **Brian on January 22, 2004 02:01 AM**

It's also important to strengthen our communities by unleashing the compassion of America's religious institutions. Religious charities of every creed are doing some of the most vital work in our country—mentoring children, feeding the hungry, taking the hand of the lonely. Yet government has often denied social service grants and contracts to these groups, just because they have a cross or a Star of David or a crescent on the wall. By executive order, I have opened billions of dollars in grant money to competition that includes faith-based charities. Tonight I ask you to codify this into law, so people of faith can know that the law will never discriminate against them again. (Applause.)

In the past, we've worked together to bring mentors to children of prisoners, and provide treatment for the addicted, and help for the homeless. Tonight I ask you to consider another group of Americans in need of help. This year, some 600,000 inmates will be released from prison back into society. We know from long experience that if they can't find work, or a home, or help, they are much more likely to commit crime and return to prison. So tonight, I propose a four-year, $300 million prisoner re-entry initiative to expand job training and placement services, to provide transitional housing, and to help newly released prisoners get mentoring, including from faith-based groups. (Applause.) America is the land of second chance, and when the gates of the prison open, the path ahead should lead to a better life. (Applause.)

VodkaPundit by Stephen Green, January 20, 2004
SOTU 31 08:01 PM
300 million bucks to train and house ex-cons.

Cheaper than keeping them locked up, but. . .who says we won't have to do so again, anyway?

Comments

► Gotta test things out every once and a while. Things can change, crime is down; we can experiment a little. **aaron 08:04 PM**

► Besides...it's got to be cheaper if we keep 20% of them out working. Taxes alone. **Niall G. 08:04 PM**

► I think this is a good thing to try and I support the concept. However, it does feel (again) like the SOTU is just a laundry list of new ways to spend our money. **Jim 08:14 PM**

► I wouldn't mind them playing around by spending new money if they would just scrap old spending at the same time. **aaron 08:23 PM**

► This might be the most important thing he said. I'm a big supporter of rehabbing convicts so they'll work. **rrsafety 08:30 PM**

► Depending on the quality of the program the recidivism rate is from one third to half or so of that of excons that don't have transitional housing and help with a job. It's more than a fifty percent improvement when effective drug and alcohol treatment is included.

Three things make a program work. It has to last long enough for the excon to get stable on a job. It has to be inexpensive enough that he or she can save money for a decent place to live and a reliable set of wheels. The rules have to be strict enough to keep them out of trouble but not so strict that it's easier in the slammer. The ones that are rooted in the Twelve Step Programs have the best track record. **Peter 09:28 PM**

► He just got Chuck Colson's enthusiastic attention and support. one of the top three influential evangelicals in the US specializes in prison issues and you guys don't see the pander? It'll probably do some good overall but this one is politics all the way. **TM Lutas 09:47 PM**

For all Americans, the last three years have brought tests we did not ask for, and achievements shared by all. By our actions, we have shown what kind of nation we are. In grief, we have found the grace to go on. In challenge, we rediscovered the courage and daring of a free people. In victory, we have shown the noble aims and good heart of America. And having come this far, we sense that we live in a time set apart.

I've been witness to the character of the people of America, who have shown calm in times of danger, compassion for one another, and toughness for the long haul. All of us have been partners in a great enterprise. And even some of the youngest understand that we are living in historic times. Last month a girl in Lincoln, Rhode Island, sent me a letter. It began, "Dear George W. Bush. If there's anything you know, I, Ashley Pearson, age 10, can do to help anyone, please send me a letter and tell me what I can do to save our country." She added this P.S.: "If you can send a letter to the troops, please put, 'Ashley Pearson believes in you.'" (Applause.)

Calpundit by Kevin Drum, January 20, 2004

7:03—Oh no, not a letter from a child from the heartland....

Comments

► He mentioned steroids because Pete Rose bet him $100 he couldn't find a way to put it into the SOTU. Oh Oh letter from little girl part, I think I am going to cry, or gag. **lk January 20, 2004 07:03 PM**

► 7:04 PM PST. GWB 25, common sense 0. Glad I took the over on the over\under. **bobbyp 07:04 PM**

► This is so much more fun than just watching the speech. **poputonian 07:04 PM**

Tonight, Ashley, your message to our troops has just been conveyed. And, yes, you have some duties yourself. Study hard in school, listen to your mom or dad, help someone in need, and when you and your friends see a man or woman in uniform, say, "thank you." (Applause.) And, Ashley, while you do your part, all of us here in this great chamber will do our best to keep you and the rest of America safe and free. (Applause.)

Calpundit by Kevin Drum, January 20, 2004

7:05—On the other hand, I have to admit that he's able to pull off this kind of heart-tugging stuff pretty well.

Comments

- ► Everything's coming up roses! Yippee! **poputonian 07:05 PM**
- ► I wish we were all a little more like Ashley. **Jeffrey G. 07:05 PM**
- ► Red ties are in, and I have none. **lk 07:07 PM**

VodkaPundit by Stephen Green, January 20, 2004

SOTU 32 08:04 PM

OK, I'm a sap.

The letter from 10-year-old Ashley Pearson (sp?) got me all chokey in a genuine awwww moment.

Moments like that one make it easier to hold my nose and vote for the guy come November.

Comments

- ► I freely admit that I actually cried... about two things, actually... the message was touching (not only as someone who's brother in-law is THERE, but as a sentimental sap) AND he said the words "Rhode Island!" It's nice for our small, but significant state to be recognized! **Jim S on January 21, 2004 11:14 AM**

My fellow citizens, we now move forward, with confidence and faith. Our nation is strong and steadfast. The cause we serve is right, because it is the cause of all mankind. The momentum of freedom in our world is unmistakable—and it is not carried forward by our power alone. We can trust in that greater power who guides the unfolding of the years. And in all that is to come, we can know that His purposes are just and true.

May God continue to bless America. (Applause.)

Calpundit by Kevin Drum, January 20, 2004

7:06—That's it? Wow. That was surely one of the shortest and least substantive SOTUs ever. And commenter Frugal Liberal wins a prize: Bush *didn't* mention the Mars mission. I thought he would.

Overall impressions—Very light on substance, but also very optimistic and inspirational. And very much aimed at the base, with talk of drugs and marriage and faith-based charities. I have a feeling it's a speech that won't go over too well with the punditocracy but probably played pretty well at home.

Comments

► The line that drove me over the edge was, "We will not ask the rest of the world for a permission slip before we take action to defend our country." What the hell does invading Iraq have to do with our national defense? **peter j. 07:04 PM**

► Osama who? **poputonian 07:08 PM**

► Did Dick Cheney dump his glass of water on Bush? Did I see that right? **Brian G. 07:11 PM**

► Kind of queer when the president of the US feels a need to bash a bunch of fags after he's had over 500 of his soldiers die in a war that was nothing more than a family feud.

After all, Saddam tried to kill his daddy. **raj 07:20 PM**

► I'll tell you what is depressing . . . watching the knee jerk reaction from this group! I think most of you had canned responses before you even watched the speech. Unfortunately this site has become nothing but a forum for Bush Haters. Try and be a little objective. I am by no means a Bush lover but you guys are ridiculous. A little objective criticism goes a long way but you guys sound about as wacked as Dean did last night! **Lyvouch 07:22 PM**

VodkaPundit by Stephen Green, January 20, 2004

SOTU 33 08:07 PM

"...it is the cause of all mankind."

He's talking about liberty, and he's right.

That's what Bush gets about foreign policy, and it's what none of the major Democratic presidential hopefuls don't—or won't—understand.

And it's why I'll almost certainly vote for him next fall. We live in dangerous times, and it looks (so far) like he's the only serious candidate.

Now if only he were as serious—and less "Clintonian" as one MSNBC commenter just said—about domestic issues.

Comments

► I agreed with almost all your comments tonight. Good job on the near real time SOTU fisking. Don't know if anyone else was doing. Good work! **Offutt_Major 08:09 PM**

► Clintonian is exactly right. Now I understand how the Democrats were feeling about Clinton. **Fredrik Nyman 08:16 PM**

► Take health care, many people are excluded because of artificially inflated prices. Why are prices inflated? Large-scale artful negotiation. How do we stop that, artful negotiation? How do you convince people to give up their station in life? **aaron 09:21 PM**

VodkaPundit by Stephen Green, January 20, 2004
SOTU Wrap-Up to Follow 08:09 PM
33 posts in 50 minutes—I need a break.
Back in a few.

Comments

► You did in impressive job. I don't think I have seen a blog updated that quickly by a single person before. Kudos to you. **Jediflyer 08:11 PM**

► Did you note the fact that he wore a red tie instead of the "Bush Blue" tie? **Director Mitch 08:17 PM**

► Nice job. I couldn't even keep up. I'm about to do another shot of Skyy to you. **aaron 08:20 PM**

Calpundit by Kevin Drum, January 20, 2004
7:15—Hey there's more! Now we get to hear from Tom and Nancy! [Tom Daschle and Nancy Pelosi, who gave the Democratic response.] But why aren't they standing up? It's awfully hard to give a good speech sitting down.

Comments

► Can someone please point me to the 'Remove Daschle from the Leadership at All Costs' website? This guy has to go. I wonder why the Dems project an image of incredible sheepishness and dullness . . . **Peter 07:30 PM**

► *More heckling the SOTU, please.*

I was doing a tyrant watch early; There went Rumsfeld, Powell, Ashcroft; there's Bush, Cheney. **poputonian 07:32 PM**

► Can someone please order up a charisma transplant for Pelosi and Daschle? Sheesh . . . **Anarch 07:32 PM**

► Lyndon Lyvouch? Oh, my. **raj 07:39 PM**

► You are missing the point. I agree with very little of what the president proposes or does, but knee jerk reactions from people that seem like they are screaming at the TV just don't seem like they are ready to discuss anything. I mean no disrespect but step back and look at yourselves.

I am looking at what both sides have to offer. I don't see much from Dems or Reps that I like. Your demeanor is very unattractive and sounds like nothing more than wishful thinking. A desperate hope that because you wish it to be bad then people will see it as bad.

I could sit here and discuss the individual points of the speech with you but I probably wouldn't disagree with as much as you think. I also didn't think much of Pelosi and Daschle's followup. They were equally as void of substance. **Lyvouch 07:39 PM**

► Lyndon Lyvouch

Very cute Raj. **Lyvouch 07:41 PM**

VodkaPundit by Stephen Green, January 20, 2004
SOTU Response 08:17 PM

Nancy Pelosi doesn't look like she's got enough *some*thing to be delivering the Democratic response. She looks barely serious enough to sell me real estate.

And even then I'd be shopping for a different agent.

UPDATE: Tom Daschle would never make it as a salesman in the private sector, and he's too much of a priss to make it as a factory worker, or even a manager. Keep him off welfare and in the Senate!

Comments

► Damn, she's trying to bury herself and the party. **aaron 08:18 PM**

► They should get Gephardt up there. He would do a much better job. **Jediflyer 08:20 PM**

► "Let us run to the UN with our mighty tails between our legs."

"Let us be sure we respond to barn doors that are open once the horses are gone."

"Let us lead by joining the herd."

Been there...done that. **Niall G. 08:23 PM**

► Damn, more digging. Focusing on jobs! Bad, Bad news. I'm find the theories on the Household vs. Establishment studies very plausible. (I'm unemp. right now. If it wasn't for unemployment comp, I'm sure I'd find a good job fast.) **aaron 08:28 PM**

► Does the two of them grinning like gargoyles drive any of the rest of you crazy? Apparently the message they took from the Iowa caucus is "Be Cheerful." **Dave Schuler 08:29 PM**

► Holy cow.

I had to flip the channel to a Bond movie for a while after the 3rd or 4th thing Pelosi said that was just ... a lie!.

Flipped back in time to hear Daschle talk about bringing "affordable drugs from Canada." What? You mean the drugs that we make here in the U.S., and the Canadian government slaps controls on (and since Canada isn't a big enough market...eh, big deal)... That's not "affordable drugs," that's running drug companies into bankruptcy via "another" government's whim!

But most of what they were.. taking.. substantial.. liberties..with.. the.. truth... were things that MOST of the U.S. "knows." At least in my experience.

I think we just saw the Democratic party try and jump the shark. I really do. **Addison 08:34 PM**

► I think I had more fun blogging the response than the President's speech. "America must be a light to the world, not just a missile." Priceless. **Spoons 08:41 PM**

► What's that mean: a missle is a smile with another I and S. **aaron 08:49 PM**

► Pssst...you are supposed to write something about permanent tax cuts as smart politics. See post SOTU #19. **Russ Goble 08:52 PM**

► "They should get Gephardt up there. He would do a much better job." Or—more to the point—Harold Ford Jr. I wonder if he's too polite to say "I told you so" to his colleagues as he passes them in the halls daily. **M. Scott Eiland 09:01 PM**

► Cutting taxes is just right. Doesn't need discussion. When I think it through, if we cap spending, kind of like CO, we could eliminate taxes and resolve many issues. So far, the only complicating factors are providing alternate opportunities for bureaucratic slack cut loose and the effects on currencies which are pegged to the dollar. **aaron 09:10 PM**

► Watching Evan Bayh on FNC[9] (Hannity & Colmes) now. Man, he's good! The D's need more people like him. **Fredrik Nyman 09:29 PM**

► All policy questions aside... an observation of the style of this and all other SOTU responses.

When will the opposition response ever be done in front of an audience? After the applause and pagentry laden SOTU, the single (or in this case two) speaker(s) talking into a camera really hurts any attempt to hold the audience's attention.

They also should find a member who is good at preparing portions of the response as the SOTU is going on. An actual response to specific points, or pointing out deficiencies in the proposals, or topics that were avoided by the president immediately would pack a better punch. **Shawn Levasseur 09:43 PM**

► I don't think any movement towards the center is going to happen quite yet, and it remains to be seen if it will happen at all.

The dem primary voters don't want republican lite, and don't care much for foreign policy issues (other than being against the Iraq war), so I expect a lot more red meat (left-wing pandering) at least until the primary process has played out and only one candidate is left standing. What happens next is up in the air at this point; it depends on who is left standing, when it happens, and how. **Fredrik Nyman 09:49 PM**

► To me, the most telling part of this address (which was mediocre, at best) was the Democratic response. An absolute abomination. Almost self-parody.

For Nancy Pelosi to bemoan the "unilateral" nature of the current efforts in Iraq after the President specifically and literally identified something like 20 nations that have contributed blood or treasure (or both) to the same effort is so patently idiotic that he automatically wins the debate on the war question by default.

On a broader plane, it has now become crystal clear to me as to why the Democratic Party will be in the firm minority for perhaps the next 10 or 20 years, or more. The Democrats are in a self-perpetuating Catch-22.

The party has degraded to the point that they have no choice but to pander to their far-left constituents. Simply put, they need 100 percent of their base even to be competitive in state-wide or national elections. Every vote is critical. The problem, of course, is that their base espouses views that are so far out of the mainstream as to be laughable.

For example, instead of pounding the President on profligate spending for unnecessary programs, they play the same, re-hashed class warfare nonsense of rich vs. poor, and the corresponding evils of tax cuts. Ludicrous. Something like 70 percent of the electorate believes that taxes are too high (even though far less than that actually pay federal taxes).

Instead of hammering the President on pushing through an expensive federal drug entitlement during a time of fiscal mismanagement, they repeat their hackneyed calls for socialized medicine. Something like 65 percent of the electorate do not want so-called "universal health care." In fact, the last time a leading Democrat actively pursued such a program, voters responded in the very next election (Mid-terms—1994) with arguably the most comprehensive political defeat for the Democratic Party in U.S. history.

In short, they're in a conundrum from which they can't escape. If they move to the center, they alienate their base. If they appease their base, they lose the center.

Trying to win a state-wide or national election as part of the Democratic Party at this point in history is like trying to win a drag race with a car that only can accelerate in low gear, but which automatically breaks a rod unless it's run in high gear. **jtj 11:40 PM**

► With not much respect (it needs to be earned)—you guys are idiots. Gaffney—Pelosi never mentioned the UN. Why did you? Talk about a lie. Lies. I see many here characterizing what was a completely mild duo-speech between the two. I think it will play well among the undecided electorate. **Andrew I BYTE BACK on January 21, 2004 01:17 AM**

► I met Daschle in an airport once. He came up to glad hand me until I gave him a dirty look and he kept going. I think I scared him a little. He's a real little guy and he was wearing this suit with the over-sized shoulder pads. He looked ridiculous. **roux on January 21, 2004 08:21 AM**

► Daschle reminded me of the Reagan puppet in the Genesis video, all those "Hollywood pseudo-dramatic head bobs."

It truly seemed as though he had studied Reagan's speech mannerisms, which were so natural in Reagan, as well as Bartlett's speech tics, so melodramatic for a television series audience, and combined them in front of a mirror after months of practice. Final result: a political speech as given by the animators of Final Fantasy. Almost human but not quite, close enough so you can't really put your finger on what's wrong. You only know something's wrong. **Peter on January 21, 2004 08:46 AM**

► My favorite part is when the Dems applauded when W said the Patriot Act would expire and he looked at them and said but the terror threat will NOT expire. **Greg on January 21, 2004 03:35 PM**

Calpundit by Kevin Drum, January 20, 2004

7:17—Wow, Pelosi is a really bad speaker, isn't she? Totally wooden.

Comments

► I wonder if response speeches aren't simply destined to sound bad. Maybe next time a Democrat is giving the response to a SOTU (hopefully not until 2013!), you might try taping it and watching it the next day, when the psychological baggage of the pomp-and-pageantry aspect of POTUS [President of the United States] addressing Congress, with all the applause and better lighting and additional claptrap. You go from all that, to a couple of people sitting down in a closed room, with less-bright lighting and no applause to punctuate the speech and no crowd reaction for the speaker to feed from. I suspect it might play better the next day. (Well, maybe not Daschle.) **Jaquandor 07:44 PM**

Calpundit by Kevin Drum, January 20, 2004

7:20—This is about the fourth or fifth miscue from Pelosi. Has she never read from a TelePrompTer before?

Comments

► The Democratic response is always bad. I missed the whole show this year, but I remember that Gary Locke totally bombed last year. Half the speech was about his grandpa or something.

I understand why they can't put presidential candidates up there, but if they were smart they'd use somebody like John Edwards. Young, up-and-coming, telegenic, and actually good at public speaking. Surprising that they haven't thought of that concept before.

I don't know who would fit the bill though. I keep reading all this good stuff about Granholm of Michigan. Maybe Harold Ford or Russell Feingold? I dunno. **JP 07:48 PM**

► ABC lets John Kerry give the 3rd Democratic response tonight which consisted of his usual boring stump speech material. Do the other candidates get equal time? What is with that anyway? Didn't Pelosi and Dashkle score enough points in ABC's opinion? I can't believe what the media goes through to discredit the President. **Dennis Slater 07:51 PM**

Calpundit by Kevin Drum, January 20, 2004

7:21—Some good stuff about increased funding for homeland security and loose nukes. Still badly delivered, but decent points.

Calpundit by Kevin Drum, January 20, 2004

7:23—OK, it's Daschle's turn. He agrees that the state of our union really *is* strong.

Comments

► They told Pelosi and Daschle it was a "patriotism mirror" That will fool those two every time. **J Edgar 08:01 PM**

► President Bush gave a speech full of various generalities, invoked 9/11, but gave little detail as to how his proposals were to be funded. The speech also seemed to lack a focus. Bush appeared to be stating that he was going to give everyone everything they wanted, and best of all, it would require no money to do this. This was his worst State of the Union.

I am also disturbed that despite the fact that he is constantly in very learned company, no one has instructed the President that the word nuclear is not pronounced "nuc-u-lur." **Roland 08:12 PM**

► Unfortunately I don't think I'll ever hear what I'm looking for in the SOTU or response. It is mainly just for public consumption. The presentation is more important than the content. A lot of people seem to respond to general discussion that the candidates hope will present them like a leader or a statesman. Too bad for us it also means very little specifics or content.

About the only thing I draw from SOTU and response are the general directions each is taking toward next year's election. In my evaluation the President is going to continue presenting himself as someone addressing the domestic issues and at the same time fighting the war on terrorism (keeping us safe). What that means to me is that he will continue spending money on domestic programs no matter what the cost and do everything possible to keep things stable in Iraq and Afgan until after the election.

The Dems tried to paint a rosey picture despite the President. They are for the first time acknowledging that the economy is turning for the better but are pointing out everything they can possibly see that is bad about it like job creation. I can say similar things about Iraq and Homeland security. Unfortunately their speech had less substance than Bush's. They proposed no specifics. (I can't wait for some of you to scream at that one)

Bottom line is all the SOTU did was set up the line that the Dems and Reps are going to be spouting for the next 10 months. **Lyvouch 08:20 PM**

► They are rebroadcasting the speech on C-span right now. It is not only unremarkable; the speech itself is horrid and confusing. I find the mention of the steroids truly bizarre and out of place in a speech that should have concentrated on Iraq and the terror war. At times, President Bush himself seemed to barely be able to contain laughter. **Roland 08:27 PM**

► Hey, maybe it was only on ABC, but did anyone else note the expressions on the faces of the servicemen and servicewomen in the audience? I'm not talking about the Joint Chiefs, but the actual soldiers in the audience. It came as close to disgust as anything I've ever SEEN in a SOTU.

My wife picked up on it immediately (and this kind of stuff is not her thing). They literally looked sickened. I'm just wondering if we imagined it, because nobody else blogged it that I've read so far.

Like I said, was it just an ABC thing? **will6 08:32 PM**

► So the smirking chimp finally stopped flapping his chops and wiggling his tail.

My, for someone who was born with a silver foot in his mouth, he is truly inarticulate. And vile.

Republican Talibans would enjoy it, though. **raj 08:51 PM**

► The reason that response commentary pales in comparison to the SOTU bloviation should be obvious. The SOTU is held in an ornate hall full of people, at least some of whom feel it necessary to applaud at every semi-colon—or whenever the "applause" sign is illuminated.

On the other hand, the response is held in a back room somewhere. Bereft of audience. And without the ornate-ness of the SOTU hall.

The fact should be clear to any psychologist. People get cues from other people. With the SOTU, there are plenty of cues. With the response, there is nothing. **raj January 21, 2004 05:13 AM**

► Actually, one might seriously ask why the American pResident is not subjected to questioning like the British prime minister.

Whatever one thinks of Tony Blair's performances, the fact is that his policies are subjected to questioning by the opposition. On television. And he has to have some defense for his positions.

Given the fact that Shrub has had—what—a miniscule 11 press conferences, which are a pale substitute for the British questioning practice, query whether Shrub is in a position to defend his policies. **raj January 21, 2004 07:06 AM**

► As to the community college thing. Read this week's NYTimes magazine article about a poor woman. She went to college and still can't get a better job than Wal-Mart. Also read Ehrenreich's *Nickel and Dimed*.[10] **mecki January 21, 2004 07:17 AM**

► I wish I had come here last night instead of getting angry and fuming all alone. It would have been a healthier outlet for my frustration.

A word about Pelosi and another reason why I am not a Democrat. Pelosi came to her seat by way of a death-bed endorsement by Sala Burton, herself a death-bed endorsement (or at least they propped her dead husband's body up and had his hand point towards her). It seems the Democrat machine in San Francisco felt that Nancy should be rewarded for all of her good works for the national Democrat Party, and that was more important than allowing San Franciscans a real opportunity to select someone of their own choice to be Congressperson (read that: No Gays Need Apply). She turned into an okay Congressperson, but since she didn't have to get her hands dirty on her rise in politics, she never developed those natural talents like, you know, talking to real people.

I know Bush didn't talk about space, but we need to watch him closely on this anyway. How many billions is it worth to give the "contract" to Halliburton to further develop nuclear power without civilian oversight, not to mention the opportunity to exploit space for military reasons?

Don't be counting the electoral votes yet. There's a lot of work to be done between now and November. These people are evil, and they're well financed. **Ray Bridges January 21, 2004 07:55 AM**

► *Hey, maybe it was only on ABC, but did anyone else note the expressions on the faces of the servicemen and servicewomen in the audience? I'm not talking about the Joint Chiefs, but the actual soldiers in the audience. It came as close to disgust as anything I've ever SEEN in a SOTU.*

My wife picked up on it immediately (and this kind of stuff is not her thing). They literally looked sickened. I'm just wondering if we imagined it, because nobody else blogged it that I've read so far.

Like I said, was it just an ABC thing?

No, it wasn't just an ABC thing. I watched on NBC and noticed it also — a complete lack of smiles or enthusiasm from almost anyone in uniform.

But they were stony faces, not angry faces. I couldn't tell if they were truly upset by what they were hearing, or if they were simply being real (as opposed to all the politicians present who know how to smile and preen for the cameras). Even so, you'd think that if the Repubs could find some soldiers to populate the audience with, they would have found the most supportive, gung-ho of the bunch.

Or maybe they were people who'd seen action in Iraq and the administration just *thought* they'd be supportive because they couldn't imagine anything else?

Notice also how Bush addressed the notion of an American "Empire." Clearly, his speechwriters were listening to and reading all the dissenting opinions in the last few months, which makes me happy that *someone* is. There were other instances of trying to address specific criticisms, but I can't think of them offhand. But it was obvious they were paying attention to what people are saying, even if they're not paying attention to the substance of their words. **Spirit January 21, 2004 08:30 AM**

► *6:51 — Any attempt to take away Medicare prescription benefits will "meet...my...veto." Huh? Who's proposing that? Especially given that Republicans control both houses of Congress?*

The Dems should use this—"You see, even the President is worried that the Republican congress is going to gut Medicare." **jaap January 21, 2004 03:04 PM**

► The response felt like one long, boring, infomercial. In future, what about doing a speech in front of an audience that is meant to rouse? It would be a lot more interesting television and keep me, for one, from switching channels looking for commentary on the "real" speech. **catherine January 21, 2004 03:52 PM**

► I was really disappointed in the SOTU speech. I did not hear promises of free cars for everyone who needs one to get to work, promises for free houses for those who do not have one, promises for free live-in doctors and free drive-in pharmacies, promises for good paying (at least $100,000 a year) jobs for everyone who needs one, promises of free 24/7 live-in childcare for everyone with children, promises of free cash rewards for those who donate money to political campaigns, promises of free unlimited abortions, promises of free weddings for any combination of people you can think of, promises to shut down every power plant in the US, promises to destroy every dam, promises to prohibit use of any federal land by anyone for any reason, promises to provide a free college education for everyone, promises to provide live-in tutors to students that need them, promises to get every polluting truck, bus and car off the road, and promises of free mental health care professionals living at your house 24/7 if you need one like I do. Did I forget anything? All this will be paid for by taxing the rich at a flat 98.34%, taxing dividends at 85.45%, taxing capital gains at 82.23%, and taxing estates at 100%. People are suffering and we need to have the government act now to end the suffering. Especially the suffering of the children. President Bush let us down. **Dennis Slater January 22, 2004 09:10 PM**

► *Wow. That Democratic response was a bit subdued. Is Daschle a Republican double-agent or something?*

Daschle is up for reelection this year I believe and is facing running against a ticket headed by a popular president who won in SD by 60%-38% in 2000. He is going to have to hide nasty, Bush-hating, Liberal Tommy in the basement for awhile. Unless Tommy can do some bigtime stuffing of some ballot boxes on the reservations he is in for a difficult re-election bid. TD has been popular in SD because he is good at bringing home the farm related pork for the big farmers in the state. That might not be enough this time. **Dennis Slater January 22, 2004 09:31 PM**

Calpundit by Kevin Drum, January 20, 2004

7:25—Ah, something about paying for Bush's plans with *your* Social Security money. Good point. Too bad he didn't follow up on it.

7:26—Come on, guys. Now some tedious arithmetic about job losses? Sheesh.

7:29—Uh oh. A nurse in Sioux Falls with cancer....

7:30—Why is it that "response" speeches are always so bad? Is it bad speechwriters? Lack of preparation? Or what?

Anti-Idiotarian Rottweiler
Author: The Emperor Misha

January 21, 2004

www.nicedoggie.net/archives/003662.html#003662

The author of this site prefers anonymity and goes by the nom de web *"The Emperor Misha." When asked where he saw his site on the political spectrum, he said,*

The far left seems to think that I'm somewhere to the right of Hitler, whereas I myself would consider my-self a conservative "small-l" libertarian, at least that's the classification I'd use in established terms. Person-ally, I think the "Anti-Idiotarian" label fits me bet-ter, meaning that I'm in favor of reason, logic and common sense (in the purely unemotional sense of the words) and against anything that defies those, regardless of the political stripe of the offender. As you'll most likely have noticed from my post on the SOTU, and possibly from other posts if you've had the time to read them, I'm an "equal opportunity offender." :-)

SOTU Address, or "Spenda-Palooza + Some Other Stuff"

That was an interesting speech. At the end, my wallet was hurting. This President has to be the most spend-happy drunken sailor that it's ever been my distinct displeasure to fund at gunpoint.

Not that all of it was utter fiscal horror, although one DID get the impression that it couldn't be long until he announced the launch of a $600 billion dollar program to fund lingerie research for transgendered Inuit bellydancers, the only interest group that he hasn't thrown a boatload of my money at yet, there was some good stuff in there, so let's take a look. We'll jump around mercilessly and skip the obligatory filler stuff:

We have faced serious challenges together, and now we face a choice: We can go forward with confidence and resolve, or we can turn back to the dangerous illusion that terrorists are not plotting and outlaw regimes are no threat to us.

Well put, and right in the face of the mewling morons who'd rather declare the war over and go home. That IS, indeed, the choice we're facing. We can either stay the course until it's over, or we can run off like a bunch of Donks at the first sign of trouble and wait until the terrorists strike us again.

Our greatest responsibility is the active defense of the American people. Twenty-eight months have passed since September 11th, 2001—over two years without an attack on American soil.

About time somebody pointed that out. Not that it's going to change a bit of the tune coming from the defeatist bedwetters and their incessant moaning about how the war hasn't made us any safer. Twenty-eight months without a single attack sounds a lot safer to me than four planes used as cruise missiles and 3,000 civilians murdered, but then again, I'm easy to please.

Inside the United States, where the war began, we must continue to give our homeland security and law enforcement personnel every tool they need to defend us.

It would be nice if you felt the same way about airline pilots. Or the rest of us, for that matter. Giving government the necessary tools is all well and good, but government can't do the job alone, nor should they be allowed to monopolize it in a war where *all* of us are on the front lines. Giving Mineta's Morons [Norman Y. Mineta, Secretary of Transportation] more tools to frisk 87-year-old grandmas from Ohio isn't going to win the war.

America is on the offensive against the terrorists who started this war. Last March, Khalid Shaikh Mohammed, a mastermind of September the 11th, awoke to find himself in the custody of U.S. and Pakistani authorities. Last August the 11th brought the capture of the terrorist Hambali, who was a key player in the attack in Indonesia that killed over 200 people. We're tracking al Qaeda around the world, and nearly two-thirds of their known leaders have now been captured or killed.

Nice to see that pointed out as well. Especially since you'd get the impression that they'd hardly gotten a scratch if your only source of news was the lame-stream media.

Thousands of very skilled and determined military personnel are on the manhunt, going after the remaining killers who hide in cities and caves, and one by one, we will bring these terrorists to justice.

I don't want them brought to justice, Mr. President, I want them dead. All of them. No mercy. No exceptions. And preferably in a way that involves a large amount of indescribable pain.

As part of the offensive against terror, we are also confronting the regimes that harbor and support terrorists,

> Thanks, Mr. President. This cannot be said often enough: We're not merely going to kick the asses of terrorists, we're also going to kick the snot out of anybody caught helping them, including nation states.
>
> I know that that's been your policy from the start, but it's still vitally important that it's repeated often and repeated forcefully.

Since we last met in this chamber, combat forces of the United States, Great Britain, Australia, Poland and other countries enforced the demands of the United Nations, ended the rule of Saddam Hussein, and the people of Iraq are free.

> Screw the United Nitwits, they're allies of our enemies, but it's still a nice touch to remind the airheads out there that it wasn't US that came up with the demands. We (the Coalition) just happened to be the only ones willing to do something about them.

Last January, Iraq's only law was the whim of one brutal man. Today our coalition is working with the Iraqi Governing Council to draft a basic law, with a bill of rights. We're working with Iraqis and the United Nations to prepare for a transition to full Iraqi sovereignty by the end of June.

> Would you QUIT talking about the Useless Nitwits, please? The very LAST thing we or the Iraqis want is for those incompetent, dictator-loving nincompoops to get involved. The Iraqis would be better off dead. And we wouldn't be too eager to mention that June deadline, if we were you. Unless you've decided to drop Iraq in the lap of the UN no matter what, of course. We'd love to see Iraq handed over to its rightful owners, the Iraqis, as soon as humanly possible, but we'd rather stay there a year too long than a week too short.
>
> Putting a deadline on it is dangerous business, and we're seriously worried that it'll come back to bite us in the a**. Does "read my lips . . ."[11] ring a bell, Dubya?

Because of American leadership and resolve, the world is changing for the better. Last month, the leader of Libya voluntarily pledged to disclose and dismantle all of his regime's weapons of mass destruction programs, including a uranium enrichment project for nuclear weapons. Colonel Qadhafi correctly judged that his country would be better off and far more secure without weapons of mass murder.

> Nicely put. Translation: "Moammar had seen what had happened to Saddam, and he knew that the same thing could easily happen to him too."

Nine months of intense negotiations involving the United States and Great Britain succeeded with Libya, while 12 years of diplomacy with Iraq did not. And one reason is clear: For diplomacy to be effective, words must be credible, and no one can now doubt the word of America.

> One of the best parts of the address, if you ask us, and EXACTLY the kind of stuff that makes the moonbats[12] writhe and squirm: Pre-emption works, and diplomacy ain't worth squat if your opponent knows that you're never going to do anything about it if he refuses to co-operate.
>
> Elementary logic, but it DOES require an IQ slightly higher than 40 to comprehend. Leftists don't have that.
>
> The President then went on to praise our brave men and women at the business end of this war, which is right and proper. They're doing a DAMN fine job and we all owe them more than we can ever repay.

I know that some people question if America is really in a war at all. They view terrorism more as a crime, a problem to be solved mainly with law enforcement and indictments.

> ...and they're all drooling f***wits.

After the chaos and carnage of September the 11th, it is not enough to serve our enemies with legal papers. The terrorists and their supporters declared war on the United States, and war is what they got.

> Thanks for calling it what it IS. A war. It would've helped immensely if you'd asked for a declaration of such back in '01, but it's nice to be reminded that you haven't forgotten.
>
> Undoubtedly, there are also a lot of s***ty tinpot dictatorships out there that needed this reminder. We're not fooling around, you p***ants, and we WILL wipe you out if you test us.

Then follows a great summary of Saddam's crimes and what would be the case if we HADN'T removed his a** from power, ended with this:

For all who love freedom and peace, the world without Saddam Hussein's regime is a better and safer place.

We're sure that Howard "Yeaerrrghhhhh" the Duck loved to hear THAT line.

And then the most beautiful b****slap we can remember coming from the mouth of a politician in a LONG time:

Some critics have said our duties in Iraq must be internationalized. This particular criticism is hard to explain to our partners in Britain, Australia, Japan, South Korea, the Philippines, Thailand, Italy, Spain, Poland, Denmark, Hungary, Bulgaria, Ukraine, Romania, the Netherlands—(applause)—Norway, El Salvador, and the 17 other countries that have committed troops to Iraq.

This one ought to be etched into titanium ClueBat[13] and said bat ought to be applied liberally to the empty skulls of every single Idiotarian ever uttering the expression "unilateral war" EVER again.

Oh, and how's this for a nice follow-up?:

There is a difference, however, between leading a coalition of many nations, and submitting to the objections of a few. America will never seek a permission slip to defend the security of our country.

OO-RAH!!!

And that's all there is to say to that!

We also hear doubts that democracy is a realistic goal for the greater Middle East, where freedom is rare. Yet it is mistaken, and condescending, to assume that whole cultures and great religions are incompatible with liberty and self-government.

Of course it is. But the Democrats ARE the party of racism and segregation, after all, so this shouldn't really surprise anybody.

I believe that God has planted in every human heart the desire to live in freedom. And even when that desire is crushed by tyranny for decades, it will rise again.

Words to live by and, in a nutshell, the difference between the right and the loony left.

As long as the Middle East remains a place of tyranny and despair and anger, it will continue to produce men and movements that threaten the safety of America and our friends.

> . . . which is why we're addressing the REAL root causes right now. Try to explain that to a moonbat, however, then duck to avoid the splatter when his pointed head explodes.

. . . above all, we will finish the historic work of democracy in Afghanistan and Iraq, so those nations can light the way for others, and help transform a troubled part of the world.

> And there it is: The Domino Effect. And guess what? It's working.
>
> Then things went downhill, as the President reached for our wallets and began what will later be known as the Biggest Spending Spree in All of History.
>
> He started out encouragingly by listing the advantages and positive consequences of the tax cuts and then, just as he had correctly asserted that

. . . the American people are using their money far better than government would have—

> . . . he inexplicably went on to demonstrate to all of us just how badly government can f*** up finances by proceeding to throw money around in gay abandon. Talk about mixed messages.

By passing the No Child Left Behind Act, you have made the expectation of literacy the law of our country. We're providing more funding for our schools—a 36-percent increase since 2001.

> . . . and we all know how wildly successful we've been in the past, pursuing the tactic of throwing more money at the bottomless pit of ignorance and union labor that is our publik skool system, don't we?
>
> But hey, let's try it AGAIN, right? Surely 446th time's the charm.
>
> His Imperial Majesty is all in favor of accountability and testing, but it's somewhat hard for him to understand why we

have to increase publik skool give-aways by 36% to achieve that.

So tonight, I propose a series of measures called Jobs for the 21st Century.

> . . . and he goes on and on from there. Hide your wallets, because there's not a single gov't leech left behind once he's done playing Santa.
>
> First he tells us that the American people are much better at spending money than government ever could be, then he proceeds to put the responsibility for job creation and education squarely in the hands of said government.
>
> He then asked for the tax cuts to be made permanent, which stopped His Majesty briefly from banging his head against the coffee table.
>
> Then he called for an end to frivolous lawsuits and idiotic federal regulations, as well as an initiative to make us less dependent on foreign energy sources, all of which made a lot of sense and brought a smile to His Majesty's face.
>
> Not to mention a call for free and fair (fair? To us, I hope) trade and partial privatization of Social Security. He was really on a roll there for a while. But then he had to go ahead and say:

And we should limit the burden of government on this economy by acting as good stewards of taxpayers' dollars.

> ...at which point he had to take a break to find his lips after they suddenly fell off.
>
> It was just as well, because His Majesty needed some time to compose himself after a particularly violent bout of roaring laughter. "Acting as good stewards of taxpayers' dollars" indeed, BWAHAHAHAHAHAHAHAHAHAHA!!!
>
> This coming from a spendthrift that makes Bill Klinton[14] look like Uncle Scrooge. There's not an IronyMeter™ with a functioning fuse left in the entire Imperial Household, we tell you. Heck, the spare fuses that hadn't even been put in yet blew up in their boxes!

In two weeks, I will send you a budget that funds the war, protects the homeland, and meets important domestic needs, while limiting the growth in discretionary spending to less than four percent.

. . . this is where he stepped down from the podium and walked around on water for a bit. "Less than four percent?" Unfortunately for President Fuzzy Math, there *are* people in this country that didn't go to publik skools and actually learned basic math. Read this.[15]

This will require that Congress focus on priorities, cut wasteful spending, and be wise with the people's money.

This is where the address nearly ended, but the President managed to skillfully dodge the lightning bolt that suddenly appeared out of nowhere.

By doing so, we can cut the deficit in half over the next five years.

By tying your hands behind your back and hiding the keys to the Treasury, we can accomplish the same in five *weeks.*

I oppose amnesty, because it would encourage further illegal immigration, and unfairly reward those who break our laws.

By this time, everybody was expecting the lightning bolt, so nobody as much as flinched. It's amazing that he can even bring himself to lie so flagrantly. We always thought that he was a Christian. Maybe he's Episcopalian, who knows?

Listen, it's quite simple: We have, at the moment, 8 million criminals running around on the loose in our country. Your proposal means that they're no longer criminals. This is an AMNESTY, dimwit!!!

"Oh, but it isn't! You see, we're going to fine them and all."

OK, we suggest the following, then: How about we take every single person off the FBI's Most Wanted List, provided that they pay a fine. That's no "amnesty" either, then.

Not that there's a snowball's chance in Hell of the fine actually still being *in* the Bill once it has gone through the bowels of Congress, but that's a different matter entirely.

Then it was on to the next of George's Giant Give-Aways, the Free Viagra for Granny $400 billion (more likely to become a trillion before we're done) Jumbo Entitlement Program, ended with this gem of a statement:

I signed this measure proudly, and any attempt to limit the choices of our seniors, or to take away their prescription drug coverage under Medicare, will meet my veto.

Shred the First Amendment with the Incumbent Protection Act and King George can't even find the pen, but if you as much as THINK about touching his Drugapalooza Spend-a-mania, he'll veto it immediately.

Gee thanks.

The War on (Some) Drugs? Let's throw money at that too. It has worked so wonderfully in the past, after all.

> In my budget, I proposed new funding to continue our aggressive, community-based strategy to reduce demand for illegal drugs.

More Goose Creek incidents are promised. That'll teach the little b*****ds!

And while we're busy with ineffective measures, King George went on to meddle where no government meddler has meddled before, professional sports, by demanding that team owners and coaches strike down hard on steroid usage.

Wonderful. We fully expect the massive smoking and snorting of steroids in our high schools to plummet as a result.

He also promised to throw more money at schools so that they can teach our kids that the best way of avoiding sexually transmitted diseases is not to have sex at all. Perfectly true, but we somehow fail to see the point in paying the schools to tell the kids what is already common knowledge, and, at any rate, is something that the parents should've told their offspring a long time ago.

Another perfect waste of money.

He then, apparently exhausted from the spending spree, took a break to explain his opposition to gay marriage and why "marriage" and "civil union" isn't the same thing. Well, he didn't explicitly say that last part, but anybody with half a synapse still firing should be able to deduce it himself after what he DID say. He also reminded those assembled that the Defense of Marriage Act wasn't something that he'd thought up out of nowhere during one of those legendary midnight meetings in the BushCheneyHalliburtonSkull'n'Crossbones Conspiracy, but rather an idea of Kaiser Willie's dating back to '96. Nice touch.

We also enjoyed his vocal opposition to activist judges a lot. We'd have enjoyed it even MORE if we'd believed that he meant a single word of what he said, but since he gleefully clapped his hands when the Supreme Sluts shredded the 14th Amendment in Michigan,[16] just to mention one example where he missed a perfect opportunity to shut up, it's pretty obvious that he doesn't have a problem with activist judges at all.

His comments on faith-based charities were quite good too. About time that a President spoke out against the non-existent wall between church and state and pointed out the blatant unfairness in denying funding to organizations that happen to have a religion. Of course, this will only mean even MORE federal spending, but if every half-a**ed atheist organization in the country can line up at the federal trough, it is nothing short of religious persecution to deny religious organizations the same right.

Want to object to federal funding of religious charities? Fine, but then you have to cut ALL federal funding. Fine by His Majesty.

Finally, in order to make sure that no citizen's wallet is left unrobbed, he promised to throw millions at felons to help them get jobs and educations.

Can't pay tuition? Rob a 7-11 and Uncle Sam will pay it for you.

It's only fair after all, seeing as how King George has put himself in the business of rewarding criminals. Why should illegal immigrants be the only ones to benefit from his generosity with our money?

Now, if you'll excuse us, we have to go sew our remaining funds into the Imperial Mattress before Dubya comes up with another hare-brained entitlement scheme.

Orcinus
Author: David Neiwert

January 20, 2004
http://dneiwert.blogspot.com/2004_01_18_dneiwert_archive.
html#107466759817934752

David Neiwert, the blogger of Orcinus, is a journalist and the author of two books, In God's Country: The Patriot Movement and the Pacific Northwest *and* Death on the Fourth of July: Hate Crimes and the American Landscape. *He left a job at MSNBC in 2002 to finish a book, and in January 2003 he began to blog. Neiwert is both a political and media critic. "Journalists like to think of themselves as being special," he says, "but they really aren't. A lot of generalists, which is what journalists*

usually are, are really rather shallow in their depth of understanding; I like
the fact that blogging opens up journalism to average people.[17]

Pickling the SOTU
By Nitra Pickler
Associated Press Hack

In his State of the Union speech Tuesday night, President Bush declared
that "Each day, law enforcement personnel and intelligence officers are
tracking terrorist threats; analysts are examining airline passenger lists;
the men and women of our new Homeland Security Department are
patrolling our coasts and borders. And their vigilance is protecting
America," but neglected to mention that the FBI has failed to even
communicate with its own agents about domestic terrorism threats.[18]

He also told Congress that "the tax relief you passed is working,"
but neglected to mention that the nation has been losing jobs at the
rate of 22,000 a month since the package passed.[19]

Bush also declared that "We are seeking all the facts" about Iraq's
supposed weapons of mass destruction, the primary justification for
going to war, adding that "already the Kay Report identified dozens of
weapons of mass destruction-related program activities and significant
amounts of equipment that Iraq concealed from the United Nations."
But he neglected to mention that he just sent home his 400-person
squad of searchers from Iraq, since so far more weapons of mass
destruction have now been found in Texas than in Iraq.[20]

Similarly, Bush claimed that "America is pursuing a forward
strategy of freedom in the greater Middle East," but he neglected to
mention that his administration has resolutely refused to become
involved in the Palestine-Israel conflict, which lies at the heart of the
region's turmoil.

He called for Congress to "reform our immigration laws, so they
reflect our values and benefit our economy," but neglected to mention
that his immigration proposal actually would benefit only employers,
while worsening conditions for workers across the nation.

Bush promoted a new nationwide drug-testing program in schools,
saying that "tonight I propose an additional 23 million for schools that
want to use drug testing as a tool to save children's lives," but neglected

to mention that he himself would likely have been kicked out of school under such a program.

He said that "the No Child Left Behind Act is opening the door of opportunity to all of America's children," but neglected to mention that his 2004 budget would underfund the legislation by $9 billion.[21]

He declared that "our nation must defend the sanctity of marriage," but neglected to explain how allowing gays to marry violated that sanctity. Bush went on to say, "The same moral tradition that defines marriage also teaches that each individual has dignity and value in God's sight," but neglected to point out that such a principle would in itself cede the right to marry to gays.

Bush concluded his speech by saying, "May God continue to bless America," but neglected to mention that the nation has been cursed by the ineptitude of his administration since the day it was forced upon us.

Note: The above is a parody. The real Nedra Pickler[22] would have offered counterpoints to Bush's speech that had no bearing whatsoever on what he actually said. Likewise, the real Nedra Pickler's counters would have been more in the line of, ". . . but he neglected to mention that Democrats are liars and traitors in any event."

And of course, she would neglect to mention that Bush's previous State of the Union address itself contained an egregious falsehood.[23]

The American Street
Author: Tom Burka

January 20, 2004

www.reachm.com/amstreet/archives/000092.html

The American Street is a group blog founded by Kevin Hayden, a.k.a. Cowboy Kahlil, who also blogs on the ReachM High Cowboy Network Noose (http://reachm.blog-city.com/). A number of prominent liberal bloggers (including David Neiwert of Orcinus) are resident American Street bloggers. The spoof below was posted by Tom Burka, who also blogs on Opinions You Should Have (www.tomburka.com).

Network and Cable Coverage of State
of the Union More Balanced Than Ever

JOHN: We're back with more of our liberally biased and objective coverage of the President's State of the Union. Bob?

BOB: It was a masterful speech, strong and hardy—like some of Campbell's soups, John.

JOHN: I think that's right. How was the delivery? We turn to drama critic Norman Lickspittle.

LICKSPITTLE: He pronounced all the words correctly, John, and punched all the right syllables. He's ready for Hamlet.

JOHN: Exactly, I thought so. Substance, Bob?

BOB: Well, Bush did exactly what he had to do: he told the Republicans that everything was all right and it was going to continue on course and get better, and he acknowledged to the Democrats that everything was broken but he had solid plans to fix everything. He praised his strengths, or created them out of whole cloth, and glossed over or plain didn't mention his failures.

LISA GIBBLER: He was aware but not aloof, in control, but not dictatorial, confident but concerned—he struck the perfect balance, hit the perfect tone.

JOHN: He earned every single moment of applause that occurred, all 365 outbursts—

BOB: And that was just from us. Half of the Congressional Gallery applauded the speech 67 times—

JOHN: But not as heartily as we did, Bob. President Bush also adequately kindled the spark of fear in each and every American while assuring Americans that, as long as he's in office, they have nothing to be afraid of.

BOB: He reflected the mood of the country. He was complaisant, superficial, full of homilies and platitudes—one of the great State speeches ever, John.

JOHN: I don't know which awed me more the speech—or the man. They were both so, so...

BOB: Masterful?

JOHN: Yes. Now: let's hear from a conservative voice.

◆◆◆◆◆◆◆

Endnotes

[1] http://volokh.blogspot.com/2002_08_04_volokh_archive.html

[2] Link to www.vodkapundit.com/archives/004365.php

[3] Byte Back is a blog (www.dimn.blogspot.com).

[4] http://djslybri.blogspot.com/2004_01_01_djslybri_archive .html#107475937368545997.

[5] "Reports that say that something hasn't happened are always interesting to me, because as we know, there are known knowns; there are things we know we know. We also know there are known unknowns; that is to say we know there are some things we do not know. But there are also unknown unknowns—the ones we don't know we don't know."—Defense Secretary Donald Rumsfeld.

[6] The "weapons of mass destruction-related program activities" line lived on for several weeks, as liberal bloggers replaced the previous abbreviation WMD with WMDRPA.

[7] IMHO—In My Humble Opinion.

[8] Andrew Sullivan's very popular and often controversial blog—www.andrewsullivan. com. See p. 112 for Sullivan's comments on a proposed "protection of marriage" amendment.

[9] Fox News Network.

[10] Barbara Ehrenreich, *Nickel and Dimed: On (Not) Getting By in America* (New York: Henry Holt and Co., 2001).

[11] The reference is to President George W. Bush's father, President George H.W. Bush, who raised taxes after promising not to: "Read my lips. No. New. Taxes."

[12] *Moonbat*, also called a *barking moonbat*—Someone on the extreme edge of whatever their -ism happens to be. (Definition attributed to Perry de Havilland.)

[13] *Cluebat*—a metaphorical instrument used to drive home a clue.

[14] Spelling *Clinton* with a *K* is a time-honored convention of the Right. I don't know why.

[15] "This" links to an article on the Kim du Toit blog dated 1/20/2004 on federal spending; URL: www.kimdutoit.com/dr/weblog.php?id=P2569.

[16] In June 2003, the Supreme Court decided to uphold the University of Michigan's law school affirmative action policy, which favors minorities. The 14th Amendment guarantees equal protection under the law, and is thereby used to argue both for and against affirmative action policies.

[17] Daniel Oppenheimer, "One Nation, Under Blog," *The Valley Advocate*, February 5, 2004. On the web at http://valleyadvocate.com/gbase/News/content?oid=oid:52704.

[18] http://dneiwert.blogspot.com/2004_01_11_dneiwert_archive.html #107412700471234186.

[19] www.salon.com/opinion/feature/2004/01/19/no_jobs/index.html.

[20] In November 2003, a domestic terrorism investigation found a sodium cyanide bomb in the hands of three people in Texas connected with white supremicist and anti-government organizations. The story is covered here: http://cbs11tv.com/investigations/local_story_330180036.html. David Neiwert's commentary is at http://dneiwert .blogspot.com/2003_11_30_dneiwert_archive.html#107049902794836725.

[21] http://seattletimes.nwsource.com/html/opinion/2001831790_dean08.html.

[22] Nedra Pickler is an Associated Press reporter thought to be biased against Democrats. See, for example, Matthew Yglesias, "Nit Picklering," *The American Prospect* (web exclusive), January 20, 2004, www.prospect.org/webfeatures/2004/01/yglesias-m-01-20.html.

[23] This refers to an unsubstantiated claim that Saddam Hussein had sought to purchase uranium in Africa, made in the 2003 State of the Union Address.

Blogging
the Issues
Part 2: Gay Marriage

━━◆━━◆━━◆━━◆━━◆━━

HOMOSEXUAL MARRIAGE: THE ISSUE flamed into national attention in November 2003, when the Massachusetts state supreme court ruled that the state had "failed to identify any constitutionally adequate reason" to deny homosexual couples the right to marry. The ruling was in response to a suit brought by eight same-sex couples. The same court decided on February 4, 2004, that civil unions for homosexuals could not stand in as a substitute for marriage.

This is not a new issue. In 1996 Congress passed and President Clinton signed into law a Defense of Marriage Act (DoMA) that stipulated states do not have to recognize same-sex marriages legalized in other states. Although this act might appear to violate the "full faith and credit" clause of Article IV of the United States Constitution, as of this writing the Defense of Marriage Act has not been successfully challenged.

But for social conservatives, 2003 had brought frightening developments. In June, a court in the Canadian province of Ontario legalized same-sex marriages, and the United States Supreme Court struck down a Texas anti-sodomy law. The Massachusetts decision seemed the last straw.

But on February 12, 2004, San Francisco City Hall began to issue same-sex marriage licenses, by order of Mayor Gavin Newsom. Couples were soon standing in line outside City Hall to marry. On February 17, two separate state judges rejected pleas by right-wing opponents to issue an immediate injunction to stop the marriages. For social conservatives, the sky had fallen, and civilization as we know it was doomed.

And so there were blogs.

TBOGG
Author: TBogg

February 13, 2004

http://tbogg.blogspot.com/2004_02_01_tbogg_archive.html

TBogg is a liberal-leaning blogger with a wicked sense of humor.

Keeping me safe from being forced to get a divorce and marry a man . . .

I see the fear of a queer planet has caused a group of Californians to gather together and become:

The Justice League of America

. . . but that didn't work out because the name was already taken and, besides, nobody had any superpowers except for that guy who can turn his eyelids inside out, so they settled for:

Campaign for California Families

. . . which doesn't sound near as cool and the odds of a McDonalds Happy Meal tie-in with an action figure is problematic. Anyway, unbeknownst to my family and other families that I am acquainted with, the CCF is going to bat for us (as well as throwing the ball in a strong overhanded manner—like a boy, not some girly-throw, by God) and keeping homosexuals who threaten our way of living, from doing the one thing that we heterosexuals do better than them: ~~start wars~~ marriage.

> Opponents of gay marriage went to court Friday to stop an extraordinary act of ongoing civil disobedience in which San Francisco has issued nearly 100 marriage licenses to gay couples.
>
> Weddings were continuing Friday and over the long holiday weekend, despite the effort by the Campaign

for California Families to obtain a restraining order that would prevent the city from issuing more licenses or performing more ceremonies inside City Hall.

But under normal legal procedures and because of Monday's President's Day holiday, it appeared unlikely that anyone would succeed in blocking the gay marriages before Tuesday.

"Frankly, it was a brilliant strategy. They got it done. The unfortunate fact is that these people who think they are married may find out Tuesday they are not," Richard Ackerman, an attorney for the conservative group, said Friday.[1]

Meaning that they will be living in (even more) sin over the long holiday weekend in San Francisco, and, frankly, isn't that what you'd really prefer to be doing this weekend instead of going to see *50 First Dates* after dinner at Red Lobster?

Here is the leader (or as they call him: Grand Monogamous Owner of the Pure and Heterosexual Penis) of the CCF, Randy Thomasson:

RANDY THOMASSON is founder and executive director of Campaign for California Families (CCF), a nonprofit, nonpartisan family issues organization standing up for moms and dads, grandparents, children, and concerned citizens statewide. Considered one of California's top pro-family leaders, Randy is on the front lines fighting to restore family-friendly values to the nation's most influential state.

[. . .]

A steadfast defender of family-friendly values, Randy has debated anti-family spokespersons on TV and radio, and has joined popular local and national talk-show hosts on their programs, such as Roger Hedgecock, Alan Colmes, Michael Reagan, John and Ken, Warren Duffy, Al Rantel, Ken and Company and Barbara Simpson. Randy has also been a guest on Dr. James Dobson's national "Focus on the Family" radio program.

> Currently, Randy is working to mobilize California's pro-family majority to regain moral territory that has been stolen from families, and to protect the rights that citizens still have.[2]

If it's all the same with Randy (ironic name alert) I'm willing to sign over my portion of the moral territory, that was stolen from my family, to a nice gay couple. Hopefully that territory is the one currently occupied by my neighbors with the six kids all under the age of nine. I hate them.

Stupid breeders.

The Mahablog
Author: Barbara O'Brien

February 26, 2004
http://www.mahablog.com/2004.02.22_arch.html#1077793247093

On February 24, President Bush announced his support for a Constitutional Amendment that would define marriage as a strictly heterosexual institution. The Left Blogosphere was mostly opposed; the Right, however, was ambivalent. My own observations, from The Mahablog.

Very basically, there are two kinds of conservatives on today's American Right: social conservatives and political conservatives. And although they have been fellow travelers and Bush supporters for some time, they really are two very different groups with very different philosophies.

Social conservatives want to use government to enforce their vision of morality and "normalcy." They want government to ban gay marriage, abortions, most divorce, and the teaching of evolution. They want government to indoctrinate conservative Christianity through prayers in public school classrooms and various "faith-based" programs.

But political conservatives lean toward libertarianism and don't like Big Gubmint, period. They've been Bush supporters because they like his tax cut plans—they tend to be "starve the beast" proponents—and they support the war in Iraq. They are mixed on whether they approve of gay marriage—some do, possibly most do not. But they do not like people messing with the Constitution and are opposed to a gay marriage amendment. And they don't want America turned into a theocracy.

The political conservatives are increasingly disenchanted with the Bush Administration over what they see as out-of-control spending, and many are furious over his immigration "reform" proposal, even though that misbegotten idea has a snowball's chance in hell of every coming to pass. The proposed amendment is a wedge, all right, but it's one that splits Bush's base, not the Dems.

And one more thing: Are the homophobes sure they want to have their national convention in *New York City*?

AndrewSullivan
Author: Andrew Sullivan
February 24, 2004
http://andrewsullivan.com/index.php?dish_inc=archives/
2004_02_22_dish_archive.html#107764340071973047

Andrew Sullivan is a gay conservative and long-time supporter of President Bush. For Sullivan, the President's support of a marriage amendment was a wrenching blow. His response to the President's speech was the talk of the Blogosphere, read and commented on by both Left and Right.

WAR IS DECLARED: The president launched a war today against the civil rights of gay citizens and their families. And just as importantly, he launched a war to defile the most sacred document in the land. Rather than allow the contentious and difficult issue of equal marriage rights to be fought over in the states, rather than let politics and the law take their course, rather than keep the Constitution out of the culture wars, this president wants to drag the very founding document into his re-election campaign. He is proposing to remove civil rights from one group of American citizens—and do so in the Constitution itself. The message could not be plainer: these citizens do not fully belong in America. Their relationships must be stigmatized in the very Constitution itself. The document that should be uniting the country will now be used to divide it, to single out a group of people for discrimination itself, and to do so for narrow electoral purposes. Not since the horrifying legacy of Constitutional racial discrimination in this country has such a goal been even thought of, let alone pursued. Those of us who supported this president in 2000, who have backed him whole-heartedly during the war, who have endured scorn from our peers as a result, who trusted that this president was indeed a uniter rather than a divider, now know the truth.

NO MORE PROFOUND AN ATTACK: This president wants our families denied civil protection and civil acknowledgment. He wants us stigmatized not just by a law, not just by his inability even to call us by name, not by his minions on the religious right. He wants us stigmatized in the very founding document of America. There can be no more profound attack on a minority in the United States—or on the promise of freedom that America represents. That very tactic is so shocking in its prejudice, so clear in its intent, so extreme in its implications that it leaves people of good will little lee-way. This president has now made the Republican party an emblem of exclusion and division and intolerance. Gay people will now regard it as their enemy for generations—and rightly so. I knew this was coming, but the way in which it has been delivered and the actual fact of its occurrence is so deeply depressing it is still hard to absorb. But the result is clear, at least for those who care about the Constitution and care about civil rights. We must oppose this extremism with everything we can muster. We must appeal to the fair-minded center of the country that balks at the hatred and fear that much of the religious right feeds on. We must prevent this graffiti from being written on a document every person in this country should be able to regard as their own. This struggle is hard but it is also easy. The president has made it easy. He's a simple man and he divides the world into friends and foes. He has now made a whole group of Americans—and their families and their friends—his enemy. We have no alternative but to defend ourselves and our families from this attack. And we will.

David E's Fablog
Author: David Ehrenstein

September 24, 2004

http://fablog.ehrensteinland.com/archives/000102.shtml#000102

David Ehrenstein of David E's Fablog is also gay, but not a conservative. He responds to Andrew Sullivan by fisking Sullivan's post.

"You realize that this means War!" said Bugs Bunny to Elmer Fudd

Well boys and girls, the preznit has called for a Constitutional Amendment banning same-sex marriage, just as everyone knew he would. And wouldn't you just know it—The Creature From the Blog Lagoon has penned a response. (You were expecting a link? As if!)

> WAR IS DECLARED: The president launched a war today against the civil rights of gay citizens and their families. And just as importantly, he launched a war to defile the most sacred document in the land. Rather than allow the contentious and difficult issue of equal marriage rights to be fought over in the states, rather than let politics and the law take their course, rather than keep the Constitution out of the culture wars, this president wants to drag the very founding document into his re-election campaign. He is proposing to remove civil rights from one group of American citizens—and do so in the Constitution itself. The message could not be plainer: these citizens do not fully belong in America. Their relationships must be stigmatized in the very Constitution itself.

And this surprises you?

> The document that should be uniting the country will now be used to divide it, to single out a group of people for discrimination itself, and to do so for narrow electoral purposes.

So much for "I'm a uniter" eh Sully?

Not since the horrifying legacy of Constitutional racial discrimination in this country has such a goal been even thought of, let alone pursued. Those of us who supported this president in 2000, who have backed him whole-heartedly during the war, who have endured scorn from our peers as a result, who trusted that this president was indeed a uniter rather than a divider, now know the truth.

The truth was apparent from Day One. You chose to ignore it. Why you chose to ignore it is a matter of considerable speculation among politicians, activists, everyday citizens and that most despised of professional minorities, psychotherapists. Indeed Gay Republicans could have the followers of Freud—and even Lacan—up on their feet and running again. Le petit object A has never looked bigger.

NO MORE PROFOUND AN ATTACK: This president wants our families denied civil protection and civil acknowledgment. He wants us stigmatized not just by a law, not just by his inability even to call us by name, not by his minions on the religious right. He wants us stigmatized in the very founding document of America. There can be no more profound attack on a minority in the United States—or on the promise of freedom that America represents. That very tactic is so shocking in its prejudice, so clear in its intent, so extreme in its implications that it leaves people of good will little leeway.

None, actually. But I'm sure you and your Log Cabinette pals are hard at work at devising some wiggle room for yourselves.

This president has now made the Republican party an emblem of exclusion and division and intolerance. Gay people will now regard it as their enemy for generations—and rightly so.

Well when didn't we?

> I knew this was coming, but the way in which it has been delivered and the actual fact of its occurrence is so deeply depressing it is still hard to absorb.

Let's hear that again, shall we?

> "I knew this was coming."

You *knew* this was coming?

And yet you insisted on supporting this man and his unelected cabal?

> But the result is clear, at least for those who care about the Constitution and care about civil rights. We must oppose this extremism with everything we can muster. We must appeal to the fair-minded center of the country that balks at the hatred and fear that much of the religious right feeds on. We must prevent this graffiti from being written on a document every person in this country should be able to regard as their own.

In other words WE MUST JOIN THE LEFT!!!!!
Right Sully?
Hello?

> This struggle is hard but it is also easy. The president has made it easy. He's a simple man and he divides the world into friends and foes. He has now made a whole group of Americans—and their families and their friends—his enemy. We have no alternative but to defend ourselves and our families from this attack. And we will.

Really? How?

You've never attacked the Right before. You've only attacked the Left. Only the Left.

The Left was the "real problem" for us all—isn't that right Sully?

But for those of us on the Left, for those of us who started the Gay Liberation movement and continue to lead it in spite of you the struggle isn't hard at all. It's obvious. And the lines were drawn long before George W. Bush drew breath.

So whatcha gonna do, Sully?

Because your call to "war" has less resonance than anything Bugs ever said to Elmer. And in the immortal words of Daffy Duck, You're despicable.

a suivre.

Greatest Jeneration
Author: Jen

February 24, 2004
http://www.greatestjeneration.com/archives/
week_2004_02_22.php#001693

From the other side: Greatest Jeneration is a socially conservative blog.

President launches drive for Constitutional Amendment to protect marriage

Here's[3] the place to go for the whole speech, but the last two paragraphs say it all for me:

> Marriage cannot be severed from its cultural, religious and natural roots without weakening the good influence of society. Government, by recognizing and protecting marriage, serves the interests of all. Today I call upon the Congress to promptly pass, and to send to the states for ratification, an amendment to our Constitution defining and protecting marriage as a union of man and woman as husband and wife. The amendment should fully protect marriage, while leaving the state legislatures free to make their own choices in defining legal arrangements other than marriage.
>
> America is a free society, which limits the role of government in the lives of our citizens. This commitment of freedom, however, does not require the redefinition of one of our most basic social institutions. Our government should respect every person, and pro-

> tect the institution of marriage. There is no contradic-
> tion between these responsibilities. We should also
> conduct this difficult debate in a manner worthy of our
> country, without bitterness or anger.

I think it is a very sad day that things have come to this state of affairs, that our President would have to come forward and take this step, but he knows what needs to be done and is doing it.

Unfortunately, the gay "marriage" activists won't quit trying to implement the civil sanction of "same sex" and other kinds of relationships until this amendment is ratified (and perhaps not even then).

Like the Communists they admire, the Liberal Left is out to destroy this republic and every institution that makes it work, and marriage and the family are a huge part of that.

American families, all of which begin with a husband and wife, are the building blocks of this, or any, nation.

I'm sure that the Founding Fathers were weeping in Heaven today, because they never saw an America where marriage would have to be Constitutionally protected or wanted to see such an abomination (President Bush didn't look too happy even speaking of it).

Liberty doesn't mean license.

But fasten your seat belts, fellow citizens; this may be a very rough ride to preserve our Republic!

VodkaPundit
Author: Stephen Green
February 24, 2004
www.vodkapundit.com/archives/005404.php#005404

A political conservative expresses his disappointment.

(Not) The Last Straw
Let's be clear: Disappointed (but hardly shocked) as I am by President Bush's speech today, I'll still be voting for him come November. Unless, that is, by some miracle the Democrats nominate someone I could trust with sharp things.

Of course, the list of remaining Democratic contenders with that requisite has dwindled to zero. And the starting number was one. Buh-bye, Joe Lieberman.

I voted for Bush in 2000 for the simple—and sole—reason that he wasn't Al Gore. All that changed a few days after 9/11, when he stood on that pile of wreckage, loudspeaker in hand, arm around a rescue worker, and said, "I can hear you. The rest of the world hears you. And the people who knocked these buildings down will hear all of us soon."

In that one moment, I became proud of my vote for George W. Bush, and I looked forward to voting with pride for his reelection.

Now, when I pull the lever for him next fall, I'll do it the way proper Victorian women were supposed to approach sex—"Close your eyes and think of England."

Unfogged
Author: Fontana Labs

February 24, 2004
www.unfogged.com/archives/week_2004_02_22.html#001498

Armageddon III

Well, it looks like the gloves are off: Bush is endorsing a marriage amendment. …

I'm peeved. Thank God he added:

> We should also conduct this difficult debate in a matter worthy of our country, without bitterness or anger.

Translation: I'll let Racicot [Marc Racicot, chairman of President Bush's re-election campaign] and the rest go hog-wild on the homos—they'll probably photoshop a picture of John Kerry starring in "Bitanic"—but I myself will look on with bemusement.

There's a lot to say about this. We should have a long national conversation about essential and contingent features of social institutions, the way conceptual continuity through theory change is possible, about the role of religious commitments in public life, and so on. Does gay marriage change the meaning of the institution, the way interracial marriage didn't? What's "the meaning of the institution," given that, um, there isn't one? But honestly I'm too annoyed to start this right now. My hope is that this turns into a "Pat Buchanan Convenion 1992" moment for the Republican party, i.e., creates a big backlash, but that's just my cheery optimistic self shining through.

And what the hell is the difference between marriage and civil unions anyway, given that secular marriages are given, you know, full faith and credit? Is this a difference that makes a difference? Sorry to play second rate Atrios and then leave just as the conversation reaches a point where I might have something substantive to add. But it'll have to wait for a calmer moment.

Priorities & Frivolities
Author: Robert Garcia Tagorda
February 24, 2004
www.tagorda.com/archives/003034.html

The Politics of the Marriage Amendment

The issue is trickier than one might think. For one thing, even though President Bush called earlier today for a "constitutional amendment protecting marriage," he didn't specifically endorse the widely discussed Musgrave proposal or any other particular text. Those who oppose marriage amendments of all forms can take no comfort in this point. But others who could be open to supporting some version of a marriage amendment (for example, the Bainbridge or the Ponnuru proposal) can find some encouragement in the President's vagueness.

Separately, most political observers attribute Bush's move to energizing the social-conservative base. That's true, of course. But I wonder nonetheless how much John Kerry's likely nomination has to do with the strategy. As discussed here, Republicans intend to paint Kerry as a New England liberal, and their plans involve spotlighting his stance on gay marriage, especially in light of his state court's recent decisions. If John Edwards were the likely nominee, would Bush feel just as compelled to make his statement? Further, if Edwards somehow beats Kerry, would Bush ease off slightly on pushing for the amendment? It's worth pondering, I think, because the manner in which the amendment is pursued may notably be impacted by the Democratic primaries.

Marriage Amendment II
Author: Robert Garcia Tagorda
February 24, 2004
www.tagorda.com/archives/003035.php

Here Robert Tagorda responds to a post by Josh Marshall on his Talking Points Memo blog, archived on the web at www.talkingpointsmemo.com/ archives/week_2004_02_22.html#002600.

Josh Marshall remarks:

> I don't think I really have anything to add to what Andrew Sullivan said with great eloquence and fury this morning about the president's decision to put the full weight of his office behind a constitutional amendment banning not only gay marriage but even the right of states to allow their citizens to enter into civil unions which would provide the legal benefits, protections and obligations of marriage.

Does Josh have some kind of exclusive scoop on what language Bush plans to back? Because I surely haven't seen anything to suggest that Bush intends to pursue "a constitutional amendment banning not only gay marriage but even the right of states to allow their citizens to enter into civil unions which would provide the legal benefits, protections and obligations of marriage." I've only seen this *Washington Post* report:

> The president, while not endorsing any specific wording, said he wanted the amendment to define marriage as the union between a man and a woman.

He said he favored leaving the states free to define alternative arrangements and protections for couples as long as they stopped short of marriage itself.

Josh later adds:

(Scott McClellan seems to have fudged a bit on the civil unions issue. But my understanding is that the specific amendment the president is backing clearly rules out civil unions too.)

The link is to a Sullivan entry on the Musgrave proposal, which I discuss below. But here's the Post again, taking a quotation from this press briefing:

McClellan said Bush believes that legislation for such an amendment, submitted by Rep. Marilyn Musgrave (R-Colo.), "meets some of the principles" in protecting the "sanctity of marriage" between men and women. But the White House declined to embrace any particular piece of legislation in Bush's announcement.

So am I missing something here, or is Josh ascribing more positions to the White House than it has made thus far?

I think it's very important for us to be clear about where our public figures stand. It's a contentious issue enough as is. The last thing we need is to add to the murkiness.

Postscript: Granted, Bush doesn't really help matters any. Perhaps he should have come out with the specific language that he intends to support. Indeed, he may have even been vague in his announcement just to give himself wiggle room down the line, thereby politicizing the issue further.

But I don't really know much about his intentions or positions besides those that are reported. And I think we should be careful of jumping to any conclusions or being imprecise about complex legal issues, given all the controversies.

Poliblog
Author: Steven Taylor
February 24, 2004
www.poliblogger.com/poliblog/archives/002955.html

Some Thoughts on Same Sex Unions

There is a great deal to say about the same-sex marriage issue, and I must admit that I have struggled with defining my own precise position. No matter what position one takes one is likely to upset someone. I am conflicted in this sense that I have moral objections to homosexuality, but also adhere to the idea that the state (i.e., government) ought to stay out of the private lives of citizens as much as possible, especially when the private actions of citizens do no harm to others. I support, generically, the idea that the courts must often protect unpopular minority positions against the tide of majority opinion. However, I also think that one cannot wholly ignore majority opinion, especially when it is widespread. There is a need for a balancing of these two positions.

There is no doubt that the issue of same-sex marriage is made more complex by the moral and religious components that undergird the debate, especially in terms of those who are opposed to the idea of same-sex marriage.

A few bullet points to deal with some of my thoughts on this topic, as I am having trouble putting this into essay format at this time:

► I am not particularly in favor of the Federal Marriage Amendment, as I do not favor using the Constitution for specific policy. Further, I object to the idea of taking what is clearly a Reserved Power, i.e., belonging to the states, and giving it to the Federal government.

► I think that marriage is a Reserved Power (i.e., belonging to the states), and that the best way to deal with the issue of same-sex marriage is for it to be dealt with on a state-by-state basis. Now, the Full Faith and Credit clause complicates this statement, but it seems constitutionally permissible, under Article IV, for the Congress to regulate how same-sex marriage would flow across state boundaries, although I do wonder as to whether such regulations would withstand an Equal Protection attack.

► The solution, it seems to me, is civil unions sans the usage of the word "marriage." It may well be no more than semantics, but it is clearly the case that the word matters. Indeed, I struggle intellectually with precisely how to deal with "marriage" versus "civil union" and find that I have a far harder time accepting the idea of gay marriage than I do in accepting the idea of civil union. At a minimum it seems to me that it does matter that for hundreds of years that the term "marriage" has meant a union of heterosexuals, and that to change that definition by judicial fiat is not appropriate.

Really, this is a compromise that ultimately I expect a vast majority of people could accept.

► I think it a legitimate position for people to have a moral objection to homosexuality (just as it is legitimate for people to have an objection to premarital sexual relations, and a host of other behaviors). However, the question becomes what role the state ought to play in these matters. I do not see the state as having a compelling reason to have a position on homosexual behavior, per se, any more than it ought to have a position on extra-marital sex. It is possible to have a moral objection, however, without being in a position to legitimately interfere with the behavior in question—e.g., I think it is normatively better for a child's parents to be wed in most cases, yet I would hardly advocate the use of state power to ensure a wedding.

► The creation of policy that explicitly acknowledges a particular kind of relationship is significant however, and the details and nature of that recognition are important—both in terms of reconciling these issues to broader principles, such as fairness and equal protection, with deeply rooted cultural norms.

► I object to the Mayor of San Francisco flaunting the law of the state of California and I object to the short-circuiting of legitimate legislative debate on this topic by the Courts. (As I objected to Roy Moore deciding that he had the sole right to interpret the First Amendment).

► I think that arguments comparing same-sex marriage to bestiality are ludicrous, although I do have to ask, and think it a legitimate question, to ask as to whether laws banning polygamy, or even the marriage of siblings, have any moral or philosophical authority if we say that marriage is not to be defined by centuries of culture and tradition, but rather something that the courts can define as they see fit.

The Right Christian
Author: The Rev. Allen Brill
February 25, 2004
http://archive.therightchristians.org/archives/000828.html

The clash of religion with political policy always stirs up interesting results. The Right Christian is a progressive Christian blog.

A Teaching Moment

I woke up this morning seeing Bush's endorsement of a federal marriage amendment as a real blessing. His current political weakness has combined with the impatience of the Christian Right to offer us an extraordinary national teaching moment. Since those arrayed against GLBT[4] equality insist on resorting to the Bible to support their case, there will be a perhaps unprecedented focus on the scriptures and how they should be interpreted. Especially since the topic is sexual, everyone who is exposed to the debate will have an opportunity to discover just how complicated it really is to apply biblical texts to modern circumstances.

I have hope that this debate will bring a new level of maturity to American Christianity. For the past 35 years, we've heard about little other than sex from the most vocal members of the Christian community. This may be an opportunity to grow out of this adolescence so that Christians can find their voice on other issues like peace and justice once again.

It won't happen without a fearless, persistent and prophetic effort on our part. Non-Christians hope that they can win the argument based solely on liberty and separation of church and state issues. I'm skeptical about that, and even if that's correct, it only postpones the reckoning until the Right uses the next "wedge" issue to distract us. I am sorely disappointed at the choice of the established leadership of the Christian Left to duck this issue and miss this chance to accomplish real progress.

Now the time is ripe to really confront what it is to be a Christian in the postmodern era . . . We must not run from this challenge.

Daily Kos
Author: Markos Moulitsas Zúniga

February 26, 2004
www.dailykos.com/story/2004/2/26/232637/219

Daily Kos is one of the leading blogs of the Left Blogosphere.

Getting It Out of Our System

The issue of Gay Marriage is obviously the hot topic, and it's one that arouses passions on all sides (me included).

But to those of you who cry doom, that say, "You've fallen into Rove's trap!" I say chill. The issue'll pass. And probably sooner rather than later.

It's a huge issue, and one that cuts to the core of our identity as Democrats. Rove may have introduced the debate, but we are responding to the Democrats, not Rove. The Democratic contingent in the Senate has handled the issue adroitly—it doesn't matter whether they are for or against gay marriage or civil unions, they simply say that the Constitution is not the place to address the issue.

It's a simple response, and one that avoids the emotional baggage of debating the merits of the issue. There's a reason the US Supreme Court likes to decide charged issues based on procedural grounds. It delays the issue until such a time that passions are cooled, and cooler heads can prevail.

This amendment is dead. The votes aren't there in the Senate. They aren't there in the House. The cable news networks were handing the Hate Amendment's Republican backers their a**es on a platter. Then Kerry came out in favor of a Massachusetts amendment. It may be a great move politically for him, but it gave the story additional legs. And now, Bush's gambit doesn't look as political as it did just yesterday. Why, they are both supporting Gay Marriage amendments! (And damned be the differences in those amendments.) Not to mention that Kerry's endorsement was completely unnecessary. It's not as if he has a vote on the matter.

So Rove is now laughing at us, right? Democrats divided, right?

Legislatively this issue isn't going anywhere. And while we all want to discuss this issue right now, I can guarantee we'll be talking about something else in two weeks. We're going to move on, and so is the country.

Sure, Bush will talk about it in his speeches, to which Democrats should ask, "Well, why aren't the two Republican controlled chambers of Congress introducing the amendment?" Expose the Hate Amendment as a political gambit, and not only do we minimize the damage, but could potentially enrage the Right—as eager as they are for AC-TION this very second.

It's true, we have moved the debate to the left. Civil unions are a given, the battle is now over nomenclature. And it's a battle I am more than happy to cede at this time. But calls for a Constitutional Amendment are a whole different matter.

Like I've said elsewhere, if this is a litmus test, it should be a pretty darn easy one to meet. You won't see me judge candidates over their gun positions, abortion stances, free trade, or whether they think gays should be allowed to marry. Just don't seek to enshrine discrimination, of any kind, in the Constitution.

As for November, I'm confident we'll all be on the same team. But it's not November. It's February. And there's nothing wrong with speaking out about what's right and what is wrong.

It's called Democracy.

The Right Christians
Author: The Rev. Allen Brill

February 27, 2004

http://archive.therightchristians.org/archives/000834.html

The Rev. Mr. Brill of The Right Christians responds to Daily Kos:

Taking Issue with Kos: The Time IS Ripe

Kos expressed yesterday what I'm sure many progressives are feeling:

> The issue of Gay Marriage is obviously the hot topic, and it's one that arouses passions on all sides (me included). But to those of you who cry doom, that say, "You've fallen into Rove's trap!", I say chill. The issue'll pass. And probably sooner rather than later.
>
> It's a huge issue, and one that cuts to the core of our identity as Democrats. Rove may have introduced the debate, but we are responding to the Democrats, not Rove. The Democratic contingent in the Senate has handled the issue adroitly—it doesn't matter whether they are for or against gay marriage or civil unions, they simply say that the Constitution is not the place to address the issue.
>
> It's a simple response, and one that avoids the emotional baggage of debating the merits of the issue. There's a reason to the US Supreme Court likes to decide charged issues based on procedural grounds. It delays the issue until such a time that passions are cooled, and cooler heads can prevail.

Those who view this as a purely political issue wish it would go away as soon as possible and prefer to not debate it on its merits. But it's not a purely political issue. As much as secular progressives dream of a world where everyone leaves their religious views at home when they come to discuss politics in the public square, that is not where we are at this time in this country.

We have a problem with Christian fundamentalism in this nation. It's not as acute as the threat posed by Muslim fundamentalism in other parts of the world, but it has been an almost constant source of division and distraction during the past 35 years.

Modernity and globalization are producing fairly rapid social changes in our society. Fundamentalism—in America's case, Christian fundamentalism—is one fear-filled response to that change. It seeks to turn back time to an idealized, non-threatening past. But fundamentalism ultimately fails because it cannot stop the march of modernity, it can only prevent its adherents from adapting to it.

American Christianity has arrived at a very teachable moment. Choosing to base their arguments about sexual behavior on ancient biblical texts, the fundamentalist leaders risk removing the veil that has shielded the eyes of their followers from the peculiarities and difficulties of the Bible. How many younger Evangelical women will be pleased to learn for the first time about the scriptures' technical definition of "adultery" that commanded that a wife be stoned to death for sleeping with another man but allowed her husband to consort with prostitutes without sanction? How long will Christian Right spokesmen be able to warn of the bogeyman of polygamy before someone demands that they show which biblical passages actually prohibit the practice? There exists a real opportunity to free many in the fundamentalists' flock from the manipulation that has been practiced upon them.

There are few things that would produce more benefits to the progressive cause. Our political discourse has been warped for a generation by one wedge issue after another, and no one should be so foolish as to think that gay equality will be the last. Christian fundamentalism is either a problem we must address or one to which we will be subject indefinitely.

Non-fundamentalist Christians have a critical role to play in this. We are able to debate this is "on the merits" and carry the discussion to the very core of the fundamentalists' presuppositions. The outcome will surely not be that fundamentalism will disappear, but just as surely its appeal to those frightened by change will be substantially reduced.

Unfortunately, the established Christian Left has taken a pass on this issue, but there are Christian progressives who are ready to cover the "religious flank" for the movement of which we are a part. We see this marriage debate not as something we wish would go away but as an opportunity to help move American Christianity out of its prolonged adolescence toward a maturity in which the faith can again be a voice for justice and peace.

Right Wing News
Author: John Hawkins
February 24, 2004
www.rightwingnews.com/archives/week_2004_02_22.PHP#001801

Right Wing News has a socially conservative orientation.

The Politics Of Gay Marriage

I am adamantly opposed to gay marriage and I'll be going into detail about my position on the subject in an editorial that'll be released on Thursday. But today, I want to talk about the politics of the Gay Marriage Amendment that Bush is now publicly supporting.

There are more than few earnest, knowledgeable, rightward leaning bloggers, who'll tell you that the President is making a political mistake to back a Constitutional Amendment that preserves the sanctity of marriage. They usually base that contention on polls that show the country is roughly divided on the topic of a Constitutional Amendment, anecdotal evidence that comes from left leaning/Libertarian blogs & emails, and posts from the relatively small number of prominent conservatives who oppose an Amendment (for the moment at least).

However, as I said back in July of 2003, this is a good issue for W. to take on. But, how can it be if the polls are split on the issue? Well, the polls ARE NOT split on gay marriage. The voters are against it by a wide margin. In most polls I've seen on the subject lately, Americans come down against gay marriage almost 2 to 1. Furthermore, not only do the voters who are against gay marriage tend to be older and more likely to vote, I feel confident that on the whole, they are much more passionate about the issue than those who favor gay marriage. That's why even in perhaps the most liberal state in the nation, California, "61% of (the) voters . . . supported Proposition 22, a ballot initiative in 2000 that said the state would recognize marriage only between a man and a woman as valid." I can tell you with confidence that I don't believe that there is single state where Bush will be hurt more than he is helped by strongly coming out against gay marriage.

Furthermore, now that we have two clear examples, in Massachusetts and San Francisco, of radical gay activists &/or liberal judges running roughshod over the will of the voters, I think the case for a Constitutional Amendment just got much, much stronger. And if the choice is between having gay marriage imposed on states by activist judges or having the Federal govt block it via Constitutional Amendment, and it is, then the latter is a better option and much more in line with what the American people want.

Last but not least, this issue is going to energize the GOP base while weakening Kerry.

The overwhelming majority of Republicans oppose gay marriage and social conservatives and Evangelicals in particular find this to be a hot button issue. So if Bush needed a way to help fire up the base without alienating a significant number of moderates, this is it.

On the other hand, as per usual, Kerry is stuck trying to play to both sides of the issue. He says he's against gay marriage and believes "marriage is between a man and a woman," but he doesn't back a Constitutional Amendment and is criticizing Bush for going that way. That's going to be a tough position to maintain long-term because the overwhelming majority of people who are militantly pro-gay marriage are on the left and Ralph Nader, who Kerry has to worry about siphoning off his voters, supports gay marriage. Yet Kerry doesn't want to alienate the majority of voters who are opposed to gay marriage. So Kerry will need to rabidly attack the people who are fighting against gay marriage to please his base even as he portrays himself as against gay marriage to the general populace. Trying to thread that needle is going to be very difficult for Kerry and I suspect he is going to end up looking very conflicted, evasive, and hypocritical, as he attempts to pull it off.

In any case, I applaud President Bush for doing the right thing and I certainly hope and expect for him to reap the political benefits of doing so.

Whatever
Author: John Scalzi
February 24, 2004
www.scalzi.com/whatever/archives/000663.html

Blogs that allow comments enable freewheeling discussion in ways television and newspapers cannot. And it's better than talk radio—everyone gets to talk on a blog.

Yes, yes, I know. I've been tiresome about gay marriage recently. But you know, look. As soon as I got done typing the last entry, I went over to CNN's Web page to find that our president backs an amendment to our constitution which would, if passed, be the first time our government has specifically encoded into our constitution the denial of a right to a specific class of people—a class of people who will have that right by the time this constitutional amendment would pass. Which means that for the first time, America would constitutionally deprive a specific set of its citizens of a right they already enjoy (Prohibition, while stupid, was a blanket prohibition). The thought of my country doing that—and of a president suggesting it should be done—sickens me. There is nothing more hateful or contemptuous or flat-out immoral that we can do as Americans than to deprive other Americans of their rights—rights we let other Americans have.

The fact that Bush is willing to try—and decries judicial "activism" when it was an equally "activist" act by the Supreme Court that gave him the job—has pretty much erased in my mind any lingering doubts that the man is one of the worst presidents this country has had. He's maybe not James Buchanan bad, but he's definitely Warren G. Harding bad—an incompetent man led by those around him and serving the interests of the few rather than the interests of his country as a whole. And even Harding didn't have the contempt for his fellow Americans to attempt a stunt like this.

It's hard for me at the moment to find too much humor in the idea of what Bush wants us all to do—indeed, I would say that that the end result of passing a constitutional amendment to bar gays and lesbians to marry would simply make me ashamed to be married. Not because I am ashamed that I have declared to the world my intent to live my life with my wife (really, far from it), but because it explicitly says I have a constitutional right that other Americans do not, and implicitly says that I deserve that right more than other Americans, for the simple fact I choose to love someone of the opposite sex.

Well, let me be clear about this: If a constitutional right isn't good enough for every American citizen, I don't see why it's good enough for me. If this constitutional amendment were to pass, I wouldn't be getting a divorce—but you can be damned sure that I'll remember who it was who made the state of marriage in America a constitutional symbol of discrimination and inequality.

Comments

▶ He's going to lose this one, John. Right now, I'm unsure as to whether he's doing this out of conviction (for which I'd cut him slack, even if I don't sympathize—principle counts for something) or to use it as a wedge issue in an election year (for which I'd just shrug with disgust and regard him as yet another politician). But I don't think he can carry it, and I wonder whether he knows that. **rick mcginnis**

▶ Well, I also doubt it will make it out of Congress. But for me, that's not the point. The point is that as a sitting President of the United States, Bush has given his voice to the idea that some Americans should have fewer Constitutional rights than others. Whether it succeeds or not is immaterial to the fact my president is putting forward this idea. **John Scalzi**

▶ If W wants to preach to ANYONE about the integrity of the matrimonial vows, he should start with his brother Neil.

That is unless he's ok with infidelity, paternity suits & assorted Asian hotel room hookers . . . **iain**

▶ I'm having an attack of pessimism nowadays. As usual, John puts things very clearly. So will others, to various degrees of clarity—the question is, will it be heard and received by those whose votes will decide come November?

Partly due to my self-isolation (no TV, getting news from websites and weblogs mostly) I have no sense of how the wind is really blowing about such matters some days. I have been hearing optimistic things from my liberal friends. "Bush will lose," they say, "no way he'll win after what he's done to the economy/international relations/citizens' rights within the country." To which I have to ask, yes, you won't vote for him because you are aware of the damage done to all these, but how can you guarantee that there aren't more voters who can't see the damage and buy that "things are just peachy/damn furriners we don't need 'em anyway/ we're at War against terrorism"?

To get back to the subject at hand, we are all aware that a constitutional amendment of that sort is legally and morally opening a can of worms bigger than one of those sixty-pound bags of dog food, only, the worms have teeth, can see, can move fast and are both vicious and poisonous.

Does that message get through?

Or will enough people not see this as such an issue, but merely a homosexuality-rights related issue?

Convince me that my pessimism is unfounded . . . please?

(Of course, the distinction is further murky because, yes, this is a homosexuality-rights issue. It's only that this particular aspect of it—a constitutional amendment—makes it much much wider in scope. **Zeynep Dilli**

► John, I think you're being overly heavy-handed in blaming Bush for this one. Yes, he is calling for a Constitutional amendment, which is a major deal, and yes, he almost certainly has personal religious convictions for doing so. Nevertheless, he is also doing what the electorate seems to want. Recall that just a few years ago, California had the chance to enshrine gay marriage through a proposition at the ballot, and declined to do so by a substantial margin — about 60% voted against it, IIRC. And if it can't pass in one of the most liberal-minded states, I can't imagine it playing any better in Peoria.

I'm not saying the FMA is the right thing to do, nor would I expect it would have any better long-term odds than Prohibition did. But social change takes time. From slavery to civil rights was a span of over 150 years. The debate on suffrage for women lasted 70. It could be that gay rights needs more time than the 30 years it's had at the fore for full acceptance. **gerrymander**

► Gerrymander writes: "I think you're being overly heavy-handed in blaming Bush for this one." I'm not blaming him for the amendment—other people did the work for on that—I'm blaming him for "supporting" the amendment. Regardless of how many people seem to think such an amendment is a good idea, it offends me that a sitting president is willing to sign on to curtailing the rights of certain American citizens. A president should know better. Either Bush does, and he's using this to make cheap political points, in which case I don't want him to be president, or he doesn't and he's utterly incompetent, in which case I don't want him to be president.

Philip says: "Clearly our society has in the past decided that constitutional rights aren't for everyone."

Well, yes, which is why amendments to the Constitution have consistently "enlarged" those rights—to former slaves and Indians, to women and even to people at the age of 18. This would be the first time, however, that rights are specifically taken "away" from a class of American citizens.
John Scalzi

► Despite what you're about to read, let me be clear: I oppose this proposed constitutional amendment.

However, I think Scalzi is off the mark, technically speaking. Proponents of the amendment are trying to protect the definition of marriage, thinking that the man-woman relationship is the foundation of society. I don't agree with that supposition, but I can understand that if someone does believe that, they would put up a fight to preserve it.

Strictly speaking, the amendment wouldn't deny anyone the right to marry. It would define what marriage is, thus (according to the proponents) reaffirm and strengthen the foundation of society. (Again, don't flame me. I don't believe that the institute of marriage is what carried humanity from caves to single family homes with indoor plumbing).

If the amendment went through—and I doubt it will—a gay man would have the same rights as me, a straight man. By defining marriage, I would have the right to marry a woman. The gay man would have the same rights. I would not have the right to marry a man. Neither would the gay man.

Our rights are equal.

Naturally, it's preposterous to think a gay man would want to marry a woman. Yet, the crux of that sentence is "want." We all know the difference between wants and rights, don't we?

My druthers: let men marry men. Let women marry women. I don't care, because I don't think society will crumble if we don't define marriage as a man-woman covenant. But if someone does believe that, I can understand why they would attempt to define marriage.

So, Scalzi, I'm with you. We agree on this.

But literally speaking, this amendment wouldn't be "a denial of a right to a specific class of people." **Todd**

► Todd says: "Strictly speaking, the amendment wouldn't deny anyone the right to marry."

Strictly speaking you are correct in one sense. However, in the sense that I am able to marry the person I would choose to because she happens to be of the opposite sex, while a gay man would not be able to marry the person he would choose to because he happens to be of the same sex, you are incorrect—and it is a right I have that a gay man or woman does not (or would not, in this case). **John Scalzi**

► Only 27 changes (amendments) in 200+ years. The Constitution will weather this one. It seems to especially hate morons that try to use its power for bad and not good. SSM [same-sex marriage] is coming and will be protected by the very instrument being used to destroy it. Ha. On a sidenote, I did find dark humor in that GW broadcast his anti-gay marriage statement during the Ellen DeGeneres Show. **Rick**

► gerrymander writes: "Yes, he is calling for a Constitutional amendment, which is a major deal, and yes, he almost certainly has personal religious convictions for doing so. Nevertheless, he is also doing what the electorate seems to want."

Apparently not. Latest Annenberg polls show that while a strong majority of Americans oppose gay marriage, a strong majority also opposes a constitutional amendment to prevent it. Bill

► For the people claiming that the rights would be equal under the amendment, let me ask you a question. Is it OK to propose an amendment banning interracial marriage? It's fundamentally the same argument (and states had laws on the books enacting this ban so it really did happen) since it claims what are "equal" rights in that nobody gets to marry outside their race (based on whatever magical formula you pulled out of your a**—but that's a different issue).

There's also the issue of States' Rights vs. Federal Rights. Historically the South should oppose this amendment on the grounds that it reduces States' Rights regardless of how distasteful "they" may find the concept of gay marriage. **Byron**

► I have heard a lot of arguments against gay marriage saying that it will ruin the "institution" of marriage, because marriage is supposed to be between a man and a woman with the purpose of procreation. So if a man and a woman want to marry, but one of them is unable to have children because of some sort of problem, then technically, according to this logic of marriage being for procreation, this couple should not be able to wed either, right? Do you see what is wrong with that logic? I certainly do. Why do people even care who marries whom? Last time I checked people didn't have to ask permission from the government to love someone. It irritates my like no other when people think that they have a say in what other citizens do, or who they "should" love. People should stay out of other people's lives! Everyone should be able to marry the person that they love! **anonymous**

► The question of "If marriage is for the purpose of having children, what about infertile couples?" came up on Ampersand's blog a while ago. Someone said it's justified by the theoretical potential. It's like a glass of water, he said. A 12-oz. glass may be empty, but it's still theoretically capable of carrying more water than a 6-oz. glass. The 12-oz. glass in this metaphor was an infertile straight couple, and the 6-oz. glass a gay couple.

A lesbian couple is perfectly capable of having a child as well. Granted, they need a little medical intervention (presuming they don't want to have intercourse with a fertile male), but it's no different from a hetero couple with fertility problems. So by that formula, we should allow lesbians to marry, at least.

What if, for instance, a male couple were to have a surrogate mother bear one (or both) of their children? Would that not also be an argument in favor of allowing gay males to marry?

I think that the main point is that, like orange juice, marriage isn't just for procreation any more. **Daniel A.**

Endnotes

[1] Associated Press, February 25, 2004 (http://www.wate.com/Global/story.asp?s=%20%201644642).

[2] www.savecalifornia.com/about/randy.cfm.

[3] White House transcript archived at www.whitehouse.gov/news/releases/2004/02/20040224-2.html.

[4] GLBT: Gay, Lesbian, Bisexual, and Transgender.

C H A P T E R   4

Best of the Blogs
Part 1: Blogging the Economy

---◆---◆---◆---◆---◆---◆---

THE QUALITY OF WRITING AND EXPERTISE on the best blogs is as good as any newspaper's op ed page, and better than most. See, for example, what bloggers can do with a dry subject—economics.

P.L.A.—A Journal of Politics, Law, and Autism
Author: Dwight Meredith
July 25, 2003
http://pla.blogspot.com/2003_07_20_pla_archive.
html#105872834433491454
Who's a big spender?
Our family lives by certain maxims promulgated by my wife. I call those maxims the "Tao of Deb." The fourth maxim of the Tao of Deb is that "the definition of interest is money they pay to us."

We are allergic to debt. We never borrow money to fund current consumption. We carry no credit card debt. We pay cash for cars and if we do not have the cash available, we drive old cars until we do.

The reasoning behind the Tao of Deb is that when money is borrowed, it must be repaid with interest. Interest payments reduce either consumption or savings. We prefer to forgo current consumption in order to maximize savings and consumption over the long run.

The same is true of government budget deficits. Those deficits are simply borrowing that must be repaid with interest. The payment of interest on the debt results either in higher taxes or lower government services.

It is not always bad for a family to borrow money. We borrowed to finance education, to buy a house and to start a business. In each of those cases, the returns were greater than the interest costs. Once we began to realize those returns, we dedicated all disposable income to pay off the debt as soon as possible.

So it also is with government borrowing. One circumstance in which it makes sense for the government to run a deficit is when the economy is falling into recession and needs a Keynesian stimulus. Like a family that incurs debt for a good reason, that debt should be quickly paid off by running a surplus when the economy is doing well. Over the economic cycle, the budget should balance.

Republicans apparently do not believe in the Tao of Deb. They run up debt to pay for current consumption in good times and bad. Of the forty-five budgets submitted from FY 1960 through FY 2004, the fifteen worst deficits[1] (as expressed by percentage of GDP) occurred under budgets submitted by Republican presidents.

Since Ronald Reagan's first budget, every budget submitted by a Republican president has resulted in a deficit. Each of those deficits was at least 2.8% of GDP except for FY 2002 when our current President was in the process of turning a surplus of 2.4% of GDP in FY 2000 into a deficit of 4.2% in FY 2003.

Many of those deficits were incurred despite the fact that the economy was doing well. In 1984, Ronald Reagan ran a deficit of 4.8% of GDP while the economy grew at a rate above 7%. George W. Bush proposes to run a deficit of $475 billion (plus the cost of operations in Iraq) next year while estimating that the economy will grow at a 3.7% clip.

From Ronald Reagan's first budget through George W. Bush's FY 2004 budget, the total debt incurred under Republican-submitted budgets is $3.54 trillion dollars. By way of comparison, the debt incurred under budgets submitted by Presidents Carter and Clinton was $192 billion, or about 1/18th of that incurred under Presidents Reagan, Bush and Bush.

How much interest do we pay each year on that $3.54 trillion? For FY 2002, we paid interest on the national debt at a rate of about 5.3%.

See here[2] and here[3] for the data from which the interest rate can be calculated.

At that rate, the interest on the debt amassed under Presidents Reagan, Bush and Bush runs about $187 billion per year. Interest on the Carter and Clinton debt is about $10 billion per year.

The House and Senate are currently in conference over a bill to add a prescription drug benefit to Medicare. The President has insisted that the price of that benefit be held to $400 billion over ten years.[4] Over the same ten-year period, we will pay more than four times that amount ($1.87 trillion) in interest on the Reagan/Bush/Bush debt.

Interest on the RBB debt is more than three times the amount the Federal government spends on education. It is larger than President Bush's 2001 tax cut (over the ten-year period of the tax cut). It is about 250 times the amount spent on autism research.

The interest on the RBB debt is greater than the combined discretionary spending for the Departments of Agriculture, Commerce, Energy, Homeland Security, Interior, Justice, Labor, Transportation, Treasury, the Corps of Engineers, EPA, the National Science Foundation, NASA, and the Small Business Administration.

President Bush is fond of reminding us that he cuts taxes because "it's your money." The debt is yours, too. There are about 100 million households in the United States. On average, each household pays $1,870 per year (or about $150 per month) for interest on the RBB debt.

It is about time that Republican presidents learned the wisdom of the Tao of Deb.

Watcher of Weasels
Author: The Watcher
January 18, 2004
www.slblogs.net/watcherofweasels/archives/000862.html

The Myth of the Jobless Recovery

We repeatedly hear Democratic hopefuls and their sympathizers in the media describing our economic recovery as a jobless one . . . sometimes going so far as to mistakenly call this the worst job market in 20 years. Unhappy with an unemployment rate that is not high enough to justify such an outrageous claim, some prefer to include part-time and temporary workers to try coming up with a "real" unemployment rate of more than 9 percent . . . but this same methodology would give you a rate as high as 12.8 percent during the Clinton administration. Though his presidency did seem to drag on forever, I seem to remember Bill Clinton being elected a bit more recently than 20 years ago.

As for the "jobless recovery" catch phrase . . . this is based on a deliberate misreading of two sets of diverging statistics put out by the Department of Labor. Employment data is gathered by the Establishment Survey, which polls 400,000 businesses on how many jobs they have filled. But the official unemployment rate itself comes from the Household Survey, which polls 60,000 homes to find out who is looking for work.

John Lott, Jr.[5] has a great article (which I found via Ipse Dixit[6]) about these statistics: "Over the last year, the Household Survey shows that almost two million new jobs have been created, while the Establishment Survey indicated a job loss of 62,000 jobs. Over the entire Bush administration, the Household Survey found that about 2.4 million new jobs have been created. By contrast, the Establishment Survey shows a net addition of only 522,000. Why the difference? The number of companies does not remain fixed. Old firms die and new ones are born. The Establishment Survey finds out about the company deaths quickly, but it takes longer to learn about births. The current list of firms surveyed excludes firms started over almost the entire last two years. What the Establishment Survey shows is that total employment in older firms has changed little over the last three years. It completely missed the growth in new jobs among new startups and self-employment."

Dick Gephardt is using Establishment Survey numbers from last August as the basis for his ridiculous claim that we have lost 3.3 million jobs, when there has actually been a net increase of at least half a million jobs. Hey, maybe Gephardt should hire someone to help him update his campaign website. He needs to update his rhetoric too . . . he was still repeating his 3.3 million nonsense while campaigning in Iowa this weekend. But at least he never went so far as Carol Moseley Braun's insanely exaggerated figure of 6 million jobs lost.[7]

We have seen unemployment fall below the average rate for the entire Clinton administration . . . and we now have an increase in jobs despite the bursting of the dot-com bubble, several corporate scandals, the 9/11 attacks, and two wars. The Democratic nominee (whoever it may be) will look like an abject idiot if, come this November, he is still using last August's numbers to argue for the repeal of Bush's tax cuts and the resurrection of Hillarycare.[8]

Who Knew?
Author: Jeremy Brown
February 15, 2004
http://whoknew.typepad.com/whoknew/
2004/02/the_tandy_indic.html

The Tandy Indicator: Good News for the Economy

I hate when the clerks in stores like Radio Shack, or auto parts and hardware stores ask me if they can help me find anything. When this happens to you, I advise you to decline. They will tell you that you can't put a 12-volt bulb in a 6-volt lamp when you know perfectly well that you can; it will just be dimmer. And maybe you *want* it dimmer because you want to use it as a reading light that won't annoy your wife as you read the collected short stories of Vladimir Nabokov at 3 in the morning while she's trying to sleep next to you. You could try saying to the clerk "well, it probably *will* work, it'll just be dimmer, which is what I want" but he will either say "Yeah but…the bulb says 12 volts and this old one you brought in says 6 volts" or he will try to sell you a bunch of parts—"you'll want this voltage variable IC power supply, this linear potentiometer with midpoint detent and on/off switch, and I recommend going with a high intensity LED, and you can etch your own circuit board…"

The two forms of "assistance" described above are equivalent in that they will make you unhappy and angry and leave you unsatisfied and bitter, but they differ completely as indicators of the state of the economy. When times are good, Radio Shack clerks—and hardware clerks, and auto parts clerks—are lousy because the good ones can get better jobs. When the economy is in the crapper, then you start to get over-qualified people—MIT grads, downsized engineers, former nuclear experts from Pakistan—helping you find your little light bulbs. I've gotten some annoyingly expert advice in these kinds of stores these past couple of years and that has made sense, since the job market has been tough. But today I tried to purchase a headlamp for my car and the guy—who insisted on using the term "dome light" which I knew to be incorrect—couldn't help me. He said they had none in stock, meaning no dome lights. I didn't have the energy to say, "you don't know what you're talking about—this is not exactly rocket science" so I walked away disappointed. But then I realized, "wait a second—it's *not* rocket science, which means this guy is *not* a rocket scientist. He doesn't know what he's doing. He doesn't really know about cars, per se. *The economy must be getting better!*" It made me feel good and I thought I'd share it with you.

Disclaimer: This blog post should in no way be taken to suggest that Radio Shack, the Tandy corporation, Aubuchon Hardware, True Value, Ace, Pep Boys, Hapco, or any other company offers anything other than exemplary service by fully qualified, courteous service professionals.

Calpundit
Author: Kevin Drum
February 23, 2004
www.calpundit.com/archives/003338.html

I've never been able to work up much interest in watching the Sunday morning chat shows, but a friend of mine who was surfing around yesterday says that the phrase "Clinton recession" was all over the place. It's the Bushies' latest talking point.

This Orwellian phrase is based on an absurd attempt to retroactively declare that the recession started in December 2000 (Clinton) instead of March 2001 (Bush), a 12-week change that obviously makes no difference to anything. But the interesting thing here isn't so much the technical arguments over the starting date of the recession as the fact that Republicans are now tacitly acknowledging that the economy isn't in great shape and are flinging some mud against the wall to see if they can blame it on somebody else.

Up until now, you see, their favored storyline has been to deny that there's really anything wrong. For months conservative commenters have been peddling an endless supply of theories designed to demonstrate that the official employment figures are wrong and the economy is really doing much better than anyone thinks. The official numbers, they said, don't pick up job gains from small firms; don't pick up job gains from the self-employed; don't pick up job gains from outsourcing; don't pick up job gains from aesthetic professions; don't pick up *something.* Two themes are common to most of these explanations: (a) government statisticians are idiots who haven't thought of any of this and (b) the authors provide exactly zero evidence for their pet theories aside from a bit of surface plausibility and a few anecdotes.

Folks like Brad DeLong[9] and the EPI [Economic Policy Institute[10]] have been doing yeoman work demonstrating that none of these explanations hold water, and even Alan Greenspan, who has previously shown a convincing willingness to shill for the Bush administration, has thrown cold water on the notion that official statistics aren't picking up the wonders of a tax-cut driven Bush recovery. Even after trying to take into account every possible explanation, he said, what remained was that the standard government statistics are the best indicators we have. There just aren't very many new jobs being created.

And so it appears that the Bush apologists may finally be giving up on this line of attack. After all, if even Alan Greenspan won't back them up, it's pretty hopeless, isn't it?

Instead, they're going to blame it on Clinton. But this is truly a desperation tactic. It means they're admitting that the economy is pretty weak, it means they're admitting that three years of tax cuts haven't helped things much, and it means they're admitting that things aren't going to get much better between now and the election.

That's the subtext of trying to pin the blame on a guy who hasn't been president for over three years: they're running scared. And it couldn't happen to a more deserving bunch of guys.

The Angry Economist
Author: Russell Nelson

February 24, 2004

http://angry-economist.russnelson.com/mankiw.html

Gregory Mankiw, chairman of the White House Council of Economic Advisers, touched off a firestorm on February 9, 2004, when he said, "Outsourcing [of jobs] is just a new way of doing international trade" that may help the U.S. economy "in the long run." A White House economic forecast he presented to Congress that day said "When a good or service is produced more cheaply abroad it makes more sense to import it than make or provide it domestically."

Gregory Mankiw

Poor Gregory Mankiw. He points out a fundamental theorem of modern economic science, and gets excoriated for it. I refer of course to his statement that outsourcing American jobs was good for the country in the long run.

He's right.

You can practically use people's reaction to his statement as a litmus test of economic understanding. Does somebody understand the least bit of economics? If so, then they agree with Gregory. If not, then they disagree with him, often vocally and vehemently. Economic flat-earthers, I call them.

America's strength is its willingness to lose jobs. Look at all the buggy-whip jobs which don't exist anymore. Or whaling jobs. Whole careers have been eliminated. Not just some jobs, but *all* of them. Gone. Not overseas, but gone from the face of the earth. Now, if we're willing to destroy jobs, why is it such a big deal if somebody else in some other country gets that job? This whole outsourcing flap is like throwing something out, and then finding that somebody has garbage-picked it.

Okay, you can make the point that we weren't really done with those jobs. That people were still willing to do them. But here's the catch: for what wages? There is no such thing as "unemployment," and there is no such thing as "unemployment insurance." Something exists that has that name, but it is not insurance. You cannot insure against something over which you have full control. Insurance doesn't work that way. Insurance covers you against things that you *cannot* control.

The alternative to losing jobs is to keep jobs doing things that people don't want. Besides the morale problems with doing something that nobody wants, you also have a serious economic problem. You can't have *everyone* doing useless work. Somebody has to be productive to pay for those jobs are no longer needed. What happens when people in the former group move into the latter group? There's no such thing as a perpetual motion machine.

You may question my assertion that "unemployment" does not exist, particularly since you hear unemployment figures quoted weekly. Very simply, yes, there are people who choose not to work for a particular wage. They are not simply unemployed; they cannot find work for a wage of their choosing. So, it doesn't make sense to talk about "unemployment" without knowing more about the jobs that aren't being taken. If a Wall Street stockbroker cannot find a job paying $200,000/year, is he unemployed? According to the Bureau of Labor Statistics, yes, he is.

Let's take a case which might be more obvious. Let's say that a laborer earning the minimum wage becomes unemployed. The stockbroker can probably find a job by offering to work for less money. The laborer doesn't have that option. He is not unemployed by choice, but instead by fiat (and no, I don't mean that the Italian car manufacturer refuses to hire him!). The source of minimum wage unemployment is the minimum wage.

Now any non-economists must be livid. "Ask people to work for less money!!! How can you do that?? You are cruel and heartless!!" Um, no. Consider the plight of the poor unfortunate Indian worker who gets paid *far* less to work in one of those Indian call centers we've heard so much about. Instead of answering the phone as Suskana, she has to answer the phone as Susan. Instead of working during the day, she has to work when most of her countrymen are asleep (IST = +1030, as opposed to an EST of -0500. Do the math). For this onerous duty, she gets paid $2 an hour, for which no American would work, could work. The thing is that her expenses are much lower. She can eat out every day for those wages, and afford a nice three-bedroom apartment in downtown Mumbai. Wages have no meaning unless you consider what they'll buy.

An efficient economy is constantly driving down prices and profits. This seems counterintuitive to anybody who lived through the inflation of the 70s. Inflation, though, is a monetary phenomenon. While it doesn't affect every price identically or immediately, it affects all prices because it's a change in the supply of money. What matters is the amount of time that you have to work to exchange for something of value to you. That amount of work has been dropping more or less steadily for the past five centuries. It may be that this year or this decade is one in which that trend shows a temporary reversal. As Mankiw said, in the long run, it's good for US jobs to be exported overseas. What he didn't say, but which is equally true, is that it may be painful in the short term when US jobs are exported overseas. The good sense of "You do what you do best, I'll do what I do best, and we'll trade" cannot be denied . . . except by people without a good sense of economics.

TM Lutas[11] comments, making the point that social relations create pressure to assist transitions into new fields. Indeed yes, but if you try to restrict job loss or tie training to the ability to eliminate jobs, then that becomes an economic issue and worthy of criticism. Separately he points out that sometimes other countries make a gift of their wealth to us, and he claims that's a problem. Personally I think "Hey, thanks for the wealth" is an adequate response, and the louder we say it, the better.

Hector Rottweiler Jr's Web Log
Author: Curtiss Leung
February 26, 2004
www.panix.com/~hncl/HectorsJournal/archives/000324.html

Annals of Inanity: Thomas Friedman's Wish . . .

. . . has already been granted:

> I've been in India for only a few days and I am already
> thinking about reincarnation. In my next life, I want to
> be a demagogue.

> Yes, I want to be able to huff and puff about com-
> plex issues—like outsourcing of jobs to India—without
> any reference to reality.
>> —from Friedman's latest assault on logic and fact,
>> "What Goes Around . . ." [12]

Friedman, of course, is here to defend outsourcing, not bury it; while he does alight on perhaps a fact or two in the subsequent 692 words (by Microsoft Word's count; **wc -w** [using Unix] gives 703), he does not dwell upon them, instead letting his fancy take him where it will, which is a fairy-tale account of economic globalization's benefits:

> Consider one of the newest products to be outsourced to India: animation. Yes, a lot of your Saturday morning cartoons are drawn by Indian animators like JadooWorks, founded three years ago here in Bangalore. India, though, did not take these basic animation jobs from Americans. For 20 years they had been outsourced by US movie companies, first to Japan and then to the Philippines, Korea, Hong Kong and Taiwan. The sophisticated, and more lucrative, preproduction, finishing and marketing of the animated films, though, always remained in America. Indian animation companies took the business away from the other Asians by proving to be more adept at both the hand-drawing of characters and the digital painting of each frame by computer—at a lower price.

I suppose this means we can all look forward to lower prices at the box office for animated features. I can hardly wait.

> But here's where the story really gets interesting. JadooWorks has decided to produce its own animated epic about the childhood of Krishna. To write the script, though, it wanted the best storyteller it could find and outsourced the project to an Emmy Award-winning U.S. animation writer, Jeffrey Scott—for an Indian epic!

> "We are also doing all the voices with American actors in Los Angeles," says Mr. Kulkarni. And the music is being written in London. JadooWorks also creates

computer games for the global market but outsources
all the design concepts to US and British game design-
ers. All the computers and animation software at
JadooWorks have also been imported from America (HP
and IBM) or Canada, and half the staff walk around in
American-branded clothing.

If this[13] is the Jeffrey Scott that Friedman refers to, then we should
all be grateful for his new employment; there's not a credit to his name
since 1999, and he may have been reduced to selling his Emmy statu-
ette. As for the HP and IBM hardware, I suppose tact prevented
Friedman from delving into whether they or their components were
assembled in the United States, and the same goes for the "American-
branded" clothing he notes on JadooWorks' staff. I merely invite my
readers to check the labels on their computers and casualwear, and then
to draw their own conclusions about the pertinence of Friedman's
observations.

Friedman's piece is the purest nonsense, and an honest high-school
teacher in favor of unrestricted trade would have given it a C- for trying
to palm off a series of unrelated impressions as an argument. But the
standards of *The New York Times* OpEd pages are not that high. To
address the question seriously, one has to concede that yes, there are
possible benefits to free capital flows in terms of national trade accounts. Nation A may outsource jobs to Nation B where labor costs are
lower, but then Nation A can make its products available to all, including Nation B, at a lower cost, thus filling the coffers of Nation A and
Nation B in an ever-increasing virtuous circle, or something like that
(sorry if the details are off—I'm only trying to recall the more recondite
defense of outsourcing given by Brad DeLong.) The problem is that
these improved trade numbers do not necessarily entail more employment or a higher standard of living in either Nations A or B. As Max
Sawicky tartly put it:

> It is easy to rest on the notion that employment always
> recovers from job losses due to outsourcing. This is tan-
> tamount to the idea that a country always recovers from
> aerial bombing. For families directly affected by
> outsourcing, there may be no recovery. Families have

finite resources and working lives. A financial reversal can have permanent effects . . . .People do not subsist on low consumer prices; they live off wages. Doesn't one translate to the other, you might logically ask? No, it doesn't. Some people spend out of non-wage income, or spend down wealth. So a price reduction does not necessarily wash out a wage decrease.

> —from the post, "OUTSOURCING IS GOOD FOR YOU—
> Not." (Of special interest is his final paragraph.)[14]

Sawicky also touches upon, but does not address, the question of how much outsourcing can adjust overall trade imbalances. I'll give that one to the proponents of outsourcing, but it only leads me to ask: given that lower consumer prices do not adjust for losses in wages and if trade balances between nations equilibriate, then who benefits? Could it be that instead of a general rise in the standard of living, all we're seeing is capital accumulation?

Whiskey Bar
Author: Billmon
April 2, 2004
http://billmon.org/archives/001320.html#comments

Working Capital

I meant to post something earlier today about the March employment report, but the corporate geeks I work for have the choker chain pulled pretty tight around my neck right now, and it's putting a big crimp in my blogging time.

I did have a chance to look at the BLS numbers,[15] however, and I was as surprised by them as just about everyone else—including stock and bond traders. Over 300k net new jobs were reportedly created in March, the biggest monthly gain in four years. Add in the upward job revisions in February and January, and the employment picture looks considerably brighter than the one we had just a few days ago, even if the unemployment rate did tick up to 5.7%.

The surprise was magnified by the fact that the recent trend in unemployment benefits[16] has given no indication of a dramatic surge in hiring. Interestingly, while the Institute for Supply Management Index[17], released yesterday, did suggest acceleration in manufacturing hiring, the BLS says manufacturing added no jobs at all last month. Instead, payroll gains came mostly from construction, retail, health care, professional services (a catch-all that includes the legion of laid-off freelance "consultants").

Even more ironically, the BLS household survey—which up until today was being falsely touted by many conservative pundits as a more reliable job measure—shows employment *fell* slightly in March. So the *National Review* is going to have to flush a lot of comments like this one down the memory hole:

> Virtually no one cites the increase in the entrepreneur-ial army of self-employed and independent contractors who have gone to work at lower tax rates, enabling them to keep more of what they earn. This is why the unemployment rate quickly fell from 6.3 percent when the Bush tax cuts were implemented last spring to 5.6 percent today. The media is trying to discredit this drop as it is scored in the more promising household survey, rather than the more pessimistic payroll tally.[18]

Presumably, Larry Kudlow is not tearing out what little hair has left over today's awful news from the household survey. A foolish consistency, etc. etc.

However, there are more substantive signs in the March report that make me wonder just how long the good times are going to roll:

Despite the big gain in March payrolls, the index of hours worked actually declined slightly, from 99.1 to 99.

The average work week also fell, from 33.8 hours to 33.7 hours.

Average hourly earnings rose a meager 2 cents, from $15.52 to $15.54. Without the seasonal adjustment, the average wage *fell* by a nickel.

Temporary employment—sometimes a leading indicator of future hiring trends—shed 1,800 jobs last month.

Thanks to the decline in hours worked and the meager gain in hourly wages, the index of aggregate payrolls (a measure of total wage payments) barely budged in March. This means the sluggish growth in

wage and salary income seen over the past three years may not accelerate to the "normal" rate of growth typically seen in a hiring recovery.

That is, if we really *are* in a sustained hiring recovery. It's possible
employers have simply been playing a bit of catch-up to the remarkably
job-free surge of output growth we saw in the second half of 2003.
Some indicators of final demand—retail spending, factory orders, etc.
— have been softening of late, as the *Wall Street Journal* noted on
Tuesday:

> In the past several weeks, retail sales and chain-store
> sales data have been short of expectations. The du-
> rable-goods report last week didn't meet forecasts. Tax
> refunds are tracking lower than had been initially fore-
> seen . . . what the latest data are suggesting is that the
> economy isn't accelerating . . .

I don't want to overstress the dark lining on the silver cloud,
because this really is a strong report—far stronger than anything we've
seen since our beloved Dear Leader took power. Who knows? If this
keeps up, before the election he may even climb out of the hole he's
been for the past three years (latest Bush job destruction count:
1,840,000.)

But if output growth really is decelerating—which is what the final
demand statistics, and the hours worked and wages paid components of
the employment report are suggesting—then it's possible employers
may soon find themselves whipsawed a bit between rising labor costs
(particularly relatively fixed costs like health benefits) and less rapidly
rising sales revenue. This, in turn, would mean some give back on those
rapid gains in productivity and profits we've seen in the heretofore
jobless recovery. So hiring *may* soon slow down again.

On the other hand, it's also possible the big March surge in payrolls
will boost consumer and business confidence, leading to higher consumption *and* capital spending, bigger pay raises, *more* job creation,
etc.—the typical virtuous upward spiral.

There would appear to be some definite limits on how far the spiral
can climb, given America's low personal savings rate, huge federal
budget deficit, and record high current account deficit, *plus* the possibility the Federal Reserve may decide it's time to take some of the

interest-rate punch out of the punchbowl. The stock market under-stands all this, which is why after surging this morning on the job news, the Dow curbed its enthusiasm as the day wore on. The bond market, meanwhile, has become the financial equivalent of Fallujah, Iraq.

But these are signs of problems that probably will only rear their ugly heads once we get a bit further down the road. And if last month's employment report really does signal the beginning of a new trend in job creation, they are also likely to be the problems that Dear Leader will have to wrestle with in his *second* term.

◆━━◆━━◆━━◆━━◆━━◆

Endnotes

[1] www.cbo.gov/table11. FY=fiscal year.

[2] www.publicdebt.treas.gov/opd/opdint.htm.

[3] www.publicdebt.treas.gov/opd/opdpdodt.htm.

[4] As of May 2004, estimates put the actual cost of the final bill between $500 and $600 billion.

[5] John Lott, a resident scholar at the American Enterprise Institute, is described on the Blogosphere either as an eminent scholar and magnificent defender of the Second Amendment or an unethical hack with gender identity issues.

[6] www.cdharris.net/archives/003225.

[7] In a February 26 blog, economist Brad DeLong suggested projecting employment at the end of 2001 forward by the rate of trend labor force growth and comparing the result to the current level of payroll employment, "and you'll see that we are 6.2 million jobs short." Read remainder at www..j-bradford-delong.net/movable_type/2004_ar-chives/000370.html#000370.

[8] This blog was cross posted to another blog, The Axis of Weasels, at www..axisofweasels.com/blog/archives/000457.html. "Hillarycare" refers to a proposal to overhaul the health care system that was created under the management of then–First Lady Hillary Clinton during President Clinton's first term. The proposal met with rousing disapproval across the political spectrum.

[9] Brad DeLong, who among other things is a professor of economics at the University of California at Berkeley, blogs at www..j-bradford-delong.net/movable_type/Index.html.

[10] www.epinet.org.

[11] Flit, www.snappingturtle.net/jmc/tmblog/archives/003811.html.

[12] www..nytimes.com/2004/02/26/opinion/26FRIE.html?ex=1393131600&en=b1aeb4ca84ea7d67&ei=5007&partner=USERLAND.

[13] www.imdb.com/name/nm0561026/. The reference is to Jeffrey Scott's listing in "The Internet Movie Database."

[14] http://maxspeak.org/mt/archives/000148.html. Here's the referenced paragraph: "Outsourcing today debunks the common idea of a separation between 'professional' and working class. You get a specialty, you might have thought you were set for life. Uh-uh. Manufacturing workers learned this a long time ago. More are learning it now. Outsourcing discounts the value of human capital. All you have left is your labor power. The other people have the capital, the good health insurance, the vacation home, the tax-deductible $75,000 SUV. You have the house, the aging car, and your dog Santorum. If you're lucky, some kind of shaky pension fund. You're a worker. Welcome to the working class. You have nothing to lose but your credit card balances."

[15] Bureau of Labor Statistics; see ftp://ftp.bls.gov/pub/news.release/empsit.txt.

[16] www.ows.doleta.gov/press/2004/040104.html.

[17] www.napm.org/ISMReport/ROB042004.htm.

[18] Larry Kudlow, "This Recovery's Not Broken," *National Review Online,* March 28, 2004.

Best of the Blogs
Part 2: Divided We Blog

THROUGHOUT THIS BOOK, I've mentioned the dissociation between Left and Right in the Blogosphere. This section is, loosely, about partisanship. Here you will learn that lefties are spoiled, brie-eating elitist appeasers, while righties are cognitively challenged and have unresolved issues about their mothers. I think also that these blogs reveal something about the roots of partisan enmity, although such analysis is beyond the scope of *this* book.

Kim du Toit
Author: Kim du Toit

May 29, 2002
www.kimdutoit.com/dr/essays.php?id=P83

Traitors Within Our Walls

A nation can survive its fools, and even the ambitious. But it cannot survive treason from within. An enemy at the gates is less formidable, for he is known and carries his banner openly. But the traitor moves amongst those within the gate freely, his sly whispers rustling through all the alleys, heard in the very halls of government itself. For the traitor appears not a traitor; he speaks in accents familiar to his victims, and he wears their face and their arguments, he appeals to the baseness that lies deep in the hearts of all men. He rots the soul of a nation, he works secretly and unknown in the night to undermine the pillars of the city, he infects the body politic so that it can no longer resist. A murderer is less to fear.

—Marcus Tullius Cicero

Cicero's words are as true today as when he spoke them, around 45 B.C. They become even more portentous when we look at recent history for an example. Bear with me while I give one example.

I've just finished reading William Shirer's *The Collapse of the Third Republic*, in which he describes, in excruciating detail, how easily the once-mighty French Republic fell to the German invasion in World War II.

Too many people have ascribed the fall of France in 1940 to the efficiency and generalship of Hitler's Wehrmacht. In fact, the seeds of destruction were sown long before that, perhaps even before the First World War.

What most people don't realize is that France was desperately weakened by the slaughter of an entire generation of men from 1914 to 1918. Just as an injured man is vulnerable to infection unrelated to his injuries, so was France thus vulnerable. And yet, even so, the strength of the Third Republic's constitution was strong enough to have survived the First World War—but when war came again, her fall was inevitable.

For in the corridors of power, there were men who hated the Republic—hated its formation, hated its structure, and hated its Constitution. The reasons may have varied, but the end result was the same.

What were those reasons? There were some whose political ambitions had been thwarted; others hated the very essence of a republic, seeking instead to exchange it with a plebiscite or worker's state; some hated it simply because of the people who supported it; and yet others saw in its destruction the potential for personal enrichment.

So these men, these bitter little men, began to chip away at the foundations of the Third Republic. And, in retrospect, it was so simple.

The traitors were helped by an appalling democratic process, a process which allowed as many political parties as there were seats in the

Assembly and the Senate. Thus, coalitions were many, which created an unstable system of government. A vote of no-confidence would inevitably be followed by the resignation of the entire government, and the formation of a new one, sometimes without any interim popular vote. The traitors were further helped by the survival of the office-holders—last year's Minister of Justice, following the fall of yet another government, might become the Minister of Foreign Affairs for the new government. Thus, while governments came and went, the same fifty people still ran the country—but it became impossible to create any kind of viable long-term government strategy, and in this uncertainty, the traitors flourished.

Only two institutions provided any kind of stability in France during the first forty years of the 20th century: the bureaucracy of State, which allowed the mechanism of government to continue; and the Army, the savior of the country at the Marne and at Verdun. (I mean, of course, the Armed Forces in general, but for brevity I'll just use the word "Army.")

Yet even these stable institutions carried within the seeds of their own destruction: the bureaucracy was stable, but it was also inflexible, and it could not implement any change swiftly, no matter how dire the consequences; and the Army contained within it charismatic figures like Marshal Pétain, heroes of a bygone era behind whom the country could rally in times of crisis—but who were woeful naïfs politically. These heroes could be manipulated by the traitors and could provide cover for traitorous activity.

Of course, the traitors were assisted by others in their endeavors, sometimes actively, sometimes by default. Most often, these helpers were in the Press, and they likewise despised the Republic, and the Army too. More tellingly, the traitors were helped by an apathetic voting public, who wearied of constant political strife and intrigue, of seeing the same faces running government regardless of election result, and of the constant clamor in the Press detailing this or the other new scandal.

The traitors began their work by undermining the Army, by denying it the funds necessary to operate and innovate, and by ensuring that the Army maintained a pacifist, defensive mentality. Hence the Maginot Line, a massive and unnecessary drain of funds on a structure out of date the day it was completed. All this could be done, the traitors knew, behind a screen of "popular support" because the people of France were sick of war, bled white by the slaughter of 1914–1918. It also served their cause to have in place a weak and incompetent Army chief, General Gamelin. Despite overwhelming evidence of his incompetence, Gamelin stayed in power, because it suited the traitors to keep him there; his weak and misguided military strategy undermined the Army's power and ability to fight a modern war.

The traitors next turned their attention to the pillars of freedom guaranteed by the French Constitution, and little by little they chipped away at them, hiding behind the continuous confusion of new government and the apathetic electorate. Most scandalously of all, the Press showed itself to be irresponsible beyond comprehension, acting like a child given a deadly weapon, scything down established principles, and using the very freedoms guaranteed by the constitution of the Republic to weaken the Republic itself.

None of this, of course, happened in a political vacuum. Outside France, there were two different types of government the traitors could support: the Communist model of Russia, and the totalitarian dictatorships of Nazi Germany and Fascist Italy. Both had their French supporters, and both would cynically unite to defeat their common enemy of the Constitutional Republic.

France was thus divided, weak, and in no position to defend herself, so when the German Army invaded in May 1940, strategic error was compounded by fatal divisiveness, and in no time at all the Germans were able to conquer France, leaving only the rump state of Vichy France to continue.

Of course, Vichy was no republic, because in the dying hours of France's war with Germany, the intriguer Pierre Laval was able to institute (by outright lies and forgery) a totalitarian government headed by erstwhile war hero Marshal Pétain, run behind the scenes by himself and a cabal of rightwing zealots. The new government allowed that both executive and legislative power rested solely in Pétain's hands, and all individual rights under the old Constitution were permanently suspended. It is hardly surprising that Vichy began to ape its model of Hitler's Germany—Jews were rounded up, imprisoned or sent off to Germany for slave labor or execution, freedom of the Press disappeared, dissidents were summarily arrested and detained indefinitely, and the iron hand of the State began to clamp down on the French people who lived in unoccupied France.

So much for the history lesson. What does it mean for us today?

Here's what it means: the history of the fall of the Third Republic gives us an invaluable means to identify the traitors in our midst today, little more than half a century later.

And I use the word "traitors" advisably. Like the French intriguers, these are people who despise our own Republic, who would replace it with another form of government, and who will form any alliance, no matter how unholy, to achieve that end. Remember too that while these are in the main politicians, they are ably abetted by their camp followers in the Press and in the bureaucracy.

Here are the means with which to identify these modern-day traitors to our Republic:

1. The first manifestation of traitors is those who would change our government completely—in other words, replace our representative form of government with a popular one. These are people who talk the most about "the majority of the people" and mean "the majority of the voters." These are people who believe that Al Gore should have won the Presidency because more people voted for him nationwide. These are people who would seek to abolish the Electoral College and replace it with a simple plebiscite. These are people who would talk of running the country and making its laws by popular referendum rather than by popular representation. Above all, these are people who talk about America as a "democracy" rather than as a "republic," mendaciously allowing the inherent rightness of the former to be confused as an end per se, rather than as the process by which we maintain the republic.

2. The next manifestation of traitors is those who would replace our basic freedoms, either by legislation or by regulation. The most common of these can be found among people who consider the Constitution a "living document," one whose terms may have been applicable when first formulated, but which seem hopelessly archaic now. Thus, for example, we get

approval for curtailment of political expression under the guise of "campaign finance reform," curtailment of our right to be armed under the guise of "protecting the children," "ending violence" or "terrorist threat." Thus too, we get approval for principles and policies that are inimical to the future welfare of the Republic which are not only faulty in philosophy, but have been proven to be failures in practice: confiscatory taxes levied only on "the rich" through the politics of envy; State confiscation of private property for "the public good"; and regulatory oppression of rights where legislative oppression is impossible to implement. Thus, for example, while the right to bear arms is entrenched in the Constitution as a universal right, the city of Chicago can ban firearms by local fiat.

3. Another manifestation of traitors is to create disunity in the republic. In a country like France, which had an ancient culture and a single language, disunity had to be created and maintained through the political process, which as we have seen was inherently unstable. In a (largely) two-party republic like ours, this is more difficult. How then is the traitor able to create and maintain perpetual disunity and instability? By creating social division. Thus we find the common glue of communication, the English language, replaced with a multiplicity of tongues and the concomitant social irritation, all under the guise of "equality." We find likewise our common culture and heritage replaced by a policy of relativism, whereby foreign cultures are as worthy as our own, and therefore our common culture is replaced by a multiplicity of cultures, all in the name of "diversity." Of course, the natural human instinct is for conformity—we do not by nature embrace diversity—so diversity must perforce be imposed on an unwilling populace by legislation and regulation, which engenders yet more resentment and disunity.

4. Finally, we find the manifestation of traitors in those who espouse causes other than (small "r") republican ones: those who call themselves "progressives," "socialists," "communitarians," "populists," "globalists" and so on. Make

no mistake about it: all these people want to replace our Republic and its forms with another type of state, one which serves their own ambitions or goals—or, most reprehensibly, the ambitions and goals of those outside our borders. Thus we find little formal opposition to United Nations–mandated land use, under the guise of "international heritage sites." We find support for international (instead of local or national) tax authority under the guise of "uniformity" or "equality" and under the auspices of unelected bodies like the Organization for Economic Cooperation and Development (OECD). And we find support for "open borders," in the final analysis a means whereby the system can be flooded with people who owe no allegiance to our society, our laws, our culture or our heritage. Each one of these is a traitorous activity, for they would surrender our national sovereignty to strangers; aggregate them, and there should be a prima facie case for criminal arraignment, especially if these activities are performed by elected or appointed officials sworn to uphold the Constitution.

We ignore these warnings and lessons at our own peril. Remember, the final objective of our modern-day traitors is no different than that of those traitors in France during the final decades of the Third Republic: they seek to replace the republic with something else. And lest anyone think that simply desiring a different form of government is neither treason nor traitorous, it should be noted that after France was liberated by the Allies in 1944, and after a long and exhaustive trial, Pierre Laval was executed by firing squad.[1]

Matt Margolis Blog
Author: Matt Margolis

July 20, 2003
www.mattmargolis.com/blog/index.php?p=124#more-124

The Futility of Debating with Liberals

I never back down from a debate with a liberal. As futile as they may be, I find even the most pointless debate with a liberal to have entertaining and educational value.

Entertaining because they rarely make sense or base their arguments on truth.

Educational because I continually learn about how liberals formulate their arguments, I recognize their flaws, and each time, they get frustrated with my continual abundance of knowledge, which they can't counter because a) they rarely use sources for their information, and b) if they actually used sources or researched an issue, they'd discover the flaws of their own arguments.

One of the key indicators of liberal's lack of concern for sources is their actual citation of sources. As strange as that sounds, I'll attempt to explain this to clarify my words.

A simple lurking of my web site will show various arguments made by both liberals and conservatives. Liberals are quick to judge any source that counters their delicate liberal values to be biased, nonobjective, and propagandist. However, they consider their sources to be unbiased, objective.

I once used the example that if a conservative reads a book titled "Democrats Are Bad," a liberal will say that you're reading ultra right-wing propagandist lies, and then they'll tell you read "Republicans Are Bad," as if to suggest that the latter title is a bastion of objectivity and void of any bias.

To liberals, conservatives are the only ones with an axe to grind, and liberals are the ones who are flawless in their messages.

In my experiences debating with liberals, they contend victory in an argument the moment they find a source (or perhaps sources) that happen to concur with their original point of the argument. However, the rebuttal to their source is ultimately not applicable to them, for whatever reasons they choose to conjure up in the heat of the moment of the debate.

Generally speaking, liberals' arguments are emotionally driven, while conservatives' arguments are founded more in logic or facts.

This is not the exception or the rule, bur the common trend.

"Get your laws off my body! Freedom of Choice"
"End racism—support affirmative action!"
"Hate-Free Zone!"
"No Blood For Oil!"

"Your civil liberties are in jeopardy!"
"Save Main Street, stop corporate giants!"
"No more school lunches for the children!"
"Bush is a Nazi!"

These are emotionally charged arguments and slogans meant to induce an emotional response to an issue—not a clear-headed logical response based on truth.

Conservatives don't suggest telling a woman what to do with her body. Hey, if she wants to be a slut, she can. If she wants to get tattoos all over her body, she can. If she wants to dye her hair orange, she can. If she wants to kill a child, she can't. The main difference between her body and a fetus is the fact that a fetus has different DNA than her own. The ultimate intent of the "Get your laws off my body" argument is to dehumanize an unborn child and regard it as an extension of a woman's body. Biologically speaking, this is far from the truth.

Liberals who support affirmative actions are by clear-headed and logical standards doubly supporting racism. Judging anyone by the color of their skin as opposed to the content of their character is without doubt racism. By assuming a minority cannot make it on their own merit, or by assuming another person is racist and will discriminate is also racist. How can racism be obliterated by the use of racism? Is it not hypocritical to use racism as means to the end of racism?

Do people have the right to hate? Yes, ultimately they do. I can hate anyone I chose to hate, as anyone can chose to hate me. However, when someone chooses to infringe on my rights to life, liberty and the pursuit of happiness because of their hate, that is not okay.

You get point.

Emotions certainly have their place in political debate. I do not question that. However, informed decisions are the not result of ones gut emotional response to an issue.

The so-called "anti-war" movement often used "the Iraqi civilians" and "the Iraqi children" in their arguments against the war in Iraq – suggesting our government's intent was to actually kill civilians deliberately, or at the very least be careless in their attempts to overthrow Saddam Hussein's regime and kill extraordinarily large number of civilians.

However, they are the ones more likely to suggest America was to blame for the terrorist attacks on September 11, 2001. They are the "progressives" telling Americans to not "become the hate they oppose" and defend ourselves from terrorism. Yet, they don't ever point a figure at the group response for the attacks, and cry foul when the government targets individuals who fall into that same category of people in the quest to fight terrorism.

Liberals will criticize our government for not being more humanitarian by offering more aide to countries in need or liberating countries with brutal dictators, but organize protests against a Republican administration when it chooses to save a country from a brutal dictator, while simultaneously taking preemptive action to defend America from terrorism.

Liberals will wage a political war against a Republican administration for not doing anything about "the homeless problem" in the United States, but never make a peep during the administration of a Democrat.

Liberals arguments are faulty for the same reasons they claim their arguments are superior. They are biased, nonobjective and propagandist. To them, a fellow liberal's opinion is more valid than a conservative's verified factual source.

A liberal will suggest to me that I read one of their celebrated book titles, but never consider reading one of my own. I, they say, am a victim of right wing propaganda.

Certainly, this piece will prompt a liberal to say that I am guilty of the same things I am suggesting they are guilty of. At first glance, it may appear so. However, the key difference is that liberal ideals have become part of the mainstream. They infiltrate the media, public education, Hollywood, and colleges and universities, amongst others. The image and perception of conservatives is blasphemed long before most people even have a real understanding of politics. With that in mind, conservative authors and such are more offering an alternative to the vast amounts of liberal propaganda that has infested the institutions previously mentioned. Because of this fact, liberal sources are not accountable for anything, even the truth.

Think I don't know what I am talking about? Well I do. I was a victim of this.

I used to be what some would call a "liberal." I never really understood or followed politics in my youth, but I was once conditioned to believe such things like Republicans are for the rich, and Democrats are for the poor. I used to buy into the idea that cops are inherently racist and corrupt. Many years ago, I once signed an online petition to free Mumia Abu-Jamal because a friend of mine told me he was innocent. I didn't know anything about the case, but my immediate emotional reaction was to defend the rights of a falsely accused black man and condemn the evil white police force.

I was so dead wrong I am ashamed of my previous actions. I fell for the liberal trap. The moment I learned about the actual case I was so completely transformed by this that this was one of the contributing factors that lead me on the path of conservatism.

That's how liberals think. They see someone like Mumia Abu Jamal and see "White Cop" and "Black Man" and their liberal emotional response makes them see "Racist White Cop" and "Innocent Black Man."

I fell for it. Lots of people fall for it. Liberalism scams your heart; it does not educate your brain.

My instinctual, uninformed, gut reactions pushed me to liberalism. My desire for knowledge and truth led me to conservatism. Emotional responses never equal objective responses.

My journey along the political spectrum included some stops along the way to the level of conservatism today. Generally, I started off as an uninformed moderate liberal. Upon my greater understanding of the issues, I became much more centrist. My complete political reawakening happened while in college—while in the belly of the liberal beast. It wasn't because I was suddenly surrounded by conservatives and they changed my views... Contrary to that, it was the previously mentioned flaws of the liberals and their positions and arguments that solidified my position on the political spectrum.

My opinions are determined on an issue-by-issue basis. My previous political history gives me a perspective where I am able to understand how liberals reach their conclusions on an issue. Hence the reason why I've successfully converted a number of liberals to being conservative.

The tactics of liberals is virtually the same whether its your typical everyday uninformed liberal, the lefty blogger on the web, a paid activist, or even an elected official.

They always attack the person more often than addressing the issue. It can be in the form of a labeling game, to just an outright personal attack. Sometimes they resort to criticizing a conservative for things they do themselves, or for causes they don't truly believe in.

Think about it. I've heard lefties calling George W. Bush a drunk, or fault him for his daughters drinking and/or smoking pot. However, these are the same people who drink underage, get drunk, smoke pot, and push for the legalization of marijuana nonetheless. It's things like these that show you that it's not about right and wrong, it's about left and right.

Crooked Timber
Author: John Holbo

May 22, 2004
www.crookedtimber.org/archives/001810.html

Crooked Timber is a group blog with fifteen resident bloggers. John Holbo also blogs on John & Belle Have a Blog (http://examinedlife. typepad.com/johnbelle/). The "Bats Aren't Bugs" theme, introduced in a May 5, 2004 blog post,[2] refers to a Calvin and Hobbs cartoon involving made-up facts.

Bats Aren't Bugs, II: Goldberg Variation

Jonah Goldberg wishes liberals were more interested in ideas,[3] specifically the history of their own ideas. He wishes they were less "intellectually deracinated"; more like conservatives:

> Read conservative publications or attend conservative conferences and there will almost always be at least some mention of our intellectual forefathers and often a spirited debate about them. The same goes for Libertarians, at least that branch which can be called a part or partner of the conservative movement.

By contrast:

> Ask a liberal about his tradition and he will talk about deeds and efforts to remedy injustice, not ideas. This is in keeping with the legacy of William James' preference for action over thought, though I doubt most liberals know or care that this is so (while I can think of

no conservative who wouldn't be jazzed to be told his idea was "Hayekian" or "Burkean"). This is a huge tactical advantage for liberals in political battles because they can disown old ideas in ways we cannot.

That was a month ago. Since then, Mark "the Decembrist" Schmitt[4] has taken these anti-liberal allegations as the occasion for what promises to be an interesting series at TAP[5]. Matthew Yglesias[6] and Kevin Drum[7] have been trying to help, politely but firmly. And Jonah gets letters, he gets letters. From liberals. Here he sits,[8] scraping the bottom of the email barrel.

Liberals condemn themselves to repeating their mistakes by not knowing their history—even, it turns out, when it's a month old. It is a sign of the arrogance of liberals that they brag—as so many have done in their emails—that they don't "need to know what to believe" or to know history or to have a philosophy or to, in effect, know their homework. They simply know what's right . . . It is also a sign of the triumph of two strains in liberal intellectual history converging: pragmatism and intellectual radicalism (by which I mean critical legal studies and the like). Both schools of thought reject the notion that "dogma" and "tradition" are useful sources of knowledge or morality, respectively.

Thus:

Their biggest problem is they don't have a philosophy. This causes a lack of organization. This causes a lack of popular ideas. This is why the Democratic Party defines itself in such reactionary terms—blocking Republicans, creating lockboxes, yelling "stop" and "no" à la Al Gore and so on.

Four theses to be considered:
1. Liberals don't know their own intellectual history.
2. Liberals don't have a philosophy.

3. Liberalism is an arrogant, intellectually flabby, feeling-based pragmatism crossed with a strain of intellectual radicalism.
4. Liberalism is strangely reactionary.

And the correct responses are:
1. Confused; maybe a grain of truth. A mistake worth making for educational purposes.
2. Weirdly false.
3. A "bats are bugs" moment for the record books.
4. Oddly, a mix of 3 and 1. (Wouldn't have thought that was possible.)

And the explanations for these correct responses:
1. *Liberals don't know their own intellectual history.* Jacob Levy[9] makes the necessary points in response much better than I would have (and just in the nick of time, before I made a botch of it). Basically, there isn't any natural presumption that students of Rawls, say, should be up on their Croly. Yes, two forms of "liberalism," but surprisingly genealogically distinct. Lots of quite different things get called "liberalism."

I would more strongly emphasize one point Jacob makes. Goldberg knows, I am sure, that "liberal" is one of those terms with so many senses it's a wonder anyone does anything with this tool except cut themselves on it. Goldberg slices himself something fierce. He uses "liberal" to denote everyone to the left of the Republican party. This is "libruhl," in the pejorative sense, much beloved of right-wing talk radio, not remotely analytically useful. For example, "critical legal studies"—which Goldberg touches on, by way of allegedly getting in touch with one tributary of the liberal stream—is not any sort of liberalism. Critical legal studies has its intellectual roots in all that post-structural, post-modern, post-Marxist continental stuff. (See this randomly Googled up page,[10] for example. I have no idea whether it is great shakes, but a long list of the influences on critical legal studies mentions not a single liberal figure or source, which tells you the thing is maybe not paradigmatically liberal.)

If you simply can't bear not to lump everyone to the left of the Republican party together, at least don't be surprised when all these folks who don't have a lot in common haven't heard of each other. Why should they?

2. *Liberals don't have a philosophy.* Wow. Knew the term was slippery. Never actually seen it leap out of anyone's hand like that and just cut the throat. Clean. Thing of beauty, if you like that sort of thing.

The implied claim that J.S. Mill, Isaiah Berlin, John Rawls, Ronald Dworkin, so forth, don't have "philosophies" is bizarre and false. So 2) is just a weird, weird thing to say, and not even the fact that Goldberg repeatedly says he is overgeneralizing to make a point explains it, because what's the point of saying something so bizarre and false? I guess he is thinking something like: leftism is fairly intellectually bankrupt. Well, we'll file that under thesis 3) and get to it in a moment. Maybe he is saying that the Democratic party is not all fired up with ideas at the moment. They are reacting to conservatives. Which is sort of true, because the conservatives are a bunch of radical hotheads, so someone needs to be doing some conserving around the place. Liberals are the Burkeans of the welfare state, ironically. We'll file this under thesis 4) and get back to it.

Yglesias[11] interprets Goldberg as offended by the intellectually unpretentious, roll-up-the-sleeves small-p pragmatical practicality of contemporary liberalism. It isn't bold and grand and exciting enough. Some of what Goldberg says seems to fit with this. I remember Henry[12] posted about this strain of contemporary conservatism some time back—sort of antsy and excitable and easily bored and in need of spectacle and stimulation. Burke the man was supposedly that way. But Burkean philosophy is notably not in favor of such things. Well, I dunno whether this is Goldberg's thing.

The point could be that there is no significant liberal overlapping philosophical consensus (as a Rawlsian might say). I don't really see that there is a terrible failing in this area—I mean, more than usual; folks always disagree. There is significant consensus, from the tip-tops of the ivory towers on down, that the modern, liberal-democratic welfare state is a good thing and that we don't need a fundamentally different form of government. That's liberal consensus.

I think Goldberg is here again seriously hampered by his tendency to call too many things "liberal." Since a lot of the thinkers he thinks are "liberals" aren't, it is no surprise that there is no liberal consensus that includes them.

But moving along, the thing that is truly weird about saying "liberals don't have a philosophy" is that it calls forth the contrary thought "so conservatives have a philosophy," which is—in my private but highly considered opinion—one of the very last thoughts a sane and prudent conservative thinker should want to spur in his or her audience. There is of course such a thing as conservative political philosophy. Would not dream of denying it. Nevertheless, philosophically speaking, contemporary conservatism is a doctrinal dog's breakfast and a very poor advertisement for conservatism as a general outlook or temperament. (I exempt libertarianism, which is highly philosophical and admirably coherent, from this complaint.)

Contemporary conservatism looks a lot less bad a couple levels up from anything you might call "philosophy." And so, young man, if you wish to make a respectable mark as a conservative mind, by all means pursue policy wonkery and conceal the odd tangle that is your ideological root system in a forest of mid-level factual detail.

This will, of course, be regarded as grave slander by conservatives. Well, I'll just link my posts on the subject. You decide. I have argued the case at inadvisable length here,[13] taking Goldberg's colleague, David Frum, to task when he tried to get philosophical. Then I sort of tied up the frayed ends here.[14] (The latter link contains a handy link to a PDF version of the first, really really long post.)

I make a short, sharp point here.[15] And got some good comments. Basically, being in favor of "go, go!" dynamist capitalist creative destruction while standing athwart the train of history, yelling "stop" … is silly. But this is the circle you've got to square.

Then there is this point[16] that conservatives, like Goldberg, who see conservatism as a temperament are left without a justification for being conservative, because temperaments are not properly reason-giving.

Not that my posts are enough coffin nails, I admit. And not that philosophical conservatism is hopeless. Not that there isn't something wise and essential about the conservative temperament. I follow Mill and Trilling in saying so. But I do think Trilling was right when he wrote, in 1949:

> In the United States at this time liberalism is not only the dominant but even the sole intellectual tradition. For it is the plain fact that nowadays there are no conservative or reactionary ideas in general circulation. This does not mean, of course, that there is no impulse to conservatism or to reaction. Such impulses are certainly very strong, perhaps even stronger than most of us know. But the conservative impulse and the reactionary impulse do not, with some isolated and some ecclesiastical exceptions, express themselves in ideas but only in irritable mental gestures which seek to resemble ideas.

Yes, the *National Review* started up right after Trilling wrote that. And Russell Kirk. Yeah, so maybe Trilling's snark stopped being true for a time. But it's true enough today. Because Jonah Goldberg is not going to be standing athwart any trains of history, yelling "stop" anytime soon. (He hates it when Democrats yell "stop." He's not about to start.) And he is not any orthodox Kirkian, and I don't see that he's a coherently unorthodox sort either.

Let's move on to the next point, which will allow me to develop some of these others.

3. *Liberalism is an arrogant, intellectually flabby, feeling-based pragmatism crossed with a strain of intellectual radicalism.*

Okay. Now the going gets strange. Despite the fact that I'm a liberal I remember—it was a whole year ago—how Goldberg, in his wisdom, dismissed the strict need to pursue consistency in arguments about ideas. Let's start with that comparatively recent event in intellectual history.

Here's how it went.[17] Radley Balko[18] caught Goldberg out on an inconsistency. Goldberg admitted it but slipped the snare neatly: "I'm sure my position will force me into uncomfortable arguments sometimes, including alas inconsistent ones. But as I've written before consistency is often a red-herring."[19] Guess that showed Balko.

You can scroll up that page and read all the bits where Goldberg elaborated and qualified his position over the next day or so. Basically, he settled on the view that it's OK to be inconsistent, so long as you think that—on some level—you are right. No inconsistency can be true, of course, but this "doesn't mean conservative inconsistency makes us wrong, it just means we have to defend our inconsistency better." Not resolve it, please note. Defend it. Even though it can't be true. It's a Russell Kirk thing, you see: "affection for the proliferating variety and mystery of human existence."

But since you can't be just go blurting "I have an affection for the proliferating variety and mystery of human existence" at the tail end of all your self-contradictions—eventually it would cause breathing problems, which would only compound the thinking problems—you need to get yourself some intellectual forefathers. Goldberg is right, I think, that conservatives are quicker with tags like "Burkean" and "Hayekian" than liberals are with corresponding tags. But I don't think this is indicative of conservative intellectual rigor. The tags have legitimate intellectual employments, to be sure, but they are also suspiciously handy crutches for logically weak legs. If you are going to be asserting logical falsehoods a lot, as Goldberg freely admits he will be, you need to be able to make it sound more high-toned, like so:

"The Burkean wisdom of P … blah, blah, blah … The compelling Hayekian insight that -P." The way to defend contradictions "better" is to be well versed in suitable material for constructing arguments from authority. Of course, if your interlocutor has even a short-term memory for intellectual history, you may be caught out in the fallacious attempt. But it's worth a try. (Not that Burke and Hayek are exactly opposites. I'm just following up on Goldberg's own examples. Burke and Hayek disagree about a thing or two, so it is perfectly possible for B to say P and H to say -P.)

The alternative would be to try and figure out which of the contradictory ideas was false. But this is not an option available to conservatives. Goldberg grouses that it is only liberals who enjoy this "tactical advantage" of being able to "disown old ideas in ways we [conservatives] cannot." (But if you think about it—and I do recommend the practice—the ability to disown old ideas, i.e. admit past errors, is actually a prerequisite for basic intellectual hygiene. I'm sure Goldberg would admit as much in a different mood.)

And this arrogant liberal trick of admitting we are fallible, illicit as it may seem, is nothing compared to the trick employed by conservatives: being able to disown any ideas whatsoever, without giving up on them, in ways we liberals cannot. For in the kingdom of ideas, you are what you imply. But conservatives, with their Goldberg-granted license to self-contradict, are free to stipulate away inconvenient implications by the Kirkian power of "the mystery of human existence." But this amounts to stipulating away the ideas themselves, which cannot actually be separated from their implications. Irritable gestures, looks like to me.

What will Goldberg say to this? First, he will protest that he is not a knee-jerk irrationalist. He thinks consistency is important, but he has a rich appreciation of how life is complicated and general principles often step on each other's toes. So inconsistency is OK. In short, he is a pragmatist. (The other possible things he might be, leading to so much flagrant self-contradiction, are: idiot, mystic, madman, liar and hypocrite. So I think I'm being quite charitable.)

But if the abiding virtue of conservatism is, at bottom, pragmatism, how can pragmatism also be the abiding vice of liberalism, as Goldberg claims? Hmm, yes?

Come to think of it, it's a little hard to believe that "affection for the proliferating variety and mystery of human existence" is anything but a feeling you feel when you feel a feeling that feels deeply right, but you can't quite say why it isn't a contradiction. So we should add: a feelings-based pragmatism is the abiding virtue of conservatism, according to Goldberg.

And although it is possible to devise flabbier forms of pragmatism, Goldberg's version is pretty flabby. Any form of pragmatism that affirms contradictions, rather than attempting to resolve them rationally, is flabby in my opinion.

And Goldberg often describes himself as an elitist, and I think claiming to be elite on the basis of nothing better than flabby feelings is pretty arrogant.

I infer that the following is a fair sketch of Goldberg's projected conservative philosophy: an arrogant, intellectually flabby, feeling-based pragmatism crossed with a strain of intellectual radicalism. In short, he is a liberal. (Except that this isn't a very good description of liberalism, which isn't essentially a species of pragmatism at all.)

I haven't gotten to the bit about Goldberg's intellectual radicalism.

4. *Liberalism is strangely reactionary.*

This is really the start of another post, rather than a proper conclusion for this one. Anyway, whenever anyone starts accusing liberals of being reactionaries, I am reminded of a passage from Frum's book, *Dead Right.*[20]

He talks about how in the halcyon Reagan years "we thought about policy and elections so hard that we seldom stopped to think about philosophy ... we learned to limit our own speculations to what the balance of political forces at that particular moment declared feasible; we wrote articles as if they were memoranda to the president, banning the not immediately practical from our discourse." There is a paradox in this notion of impractical, speculative conservatism, if I make no mistake.

But at some point the flip was indeed made. Liberals are more conservative than conservatives, these days. Liberals are Burkeans of the welfare state. Whereas the Burkeans have all turned Jacobins, wild-eyed radicals. Hence Goldberg's frustration at liberal reactionaries, always standing athwart the train of history, shouting "stop." I quote again:

> The Democratic Party defines itself in such re-
> actionary terms—blocking Republicans, creat-
> ing lockboxes, yelling "stop" and "no" à la Al
> Gore and so on.

As a conservative, he can't abide such counter-revolutionary obstructionism.

I do realize that Goldberg himself is aware of at least some of these ironies. Whole thing is very confusing.

Comments

► I find it curious that you have such evident interest about what this low-grade journalist, who is not noticeably better informed than the vole of the field, thinks about anything.

I'm as interested in the sociology of reaction as much as anyone, but at a certain point you've got to fire up Excel, or an open-source equivalent, and run a cost-benefit analysis. **chun the unavoidable**

► For the twenty yr old engineer or programmer who shoots Klingons and wants to feel tough, this might appeal.

I just was remembering that Goldberg tried that goatee look a while back, and it reminded me of the ST episode with Spock from the parallel universe with the evil Kirk. Maybe this is where he's trying to position himself. I bet he's in front of the mirror now practicing how to arch one eyebrow. . . **liberal japonicus**

► "Typical. So typical. Savage life forms never follow even their own rules."

—[uppercase] Q, "Encounter at Farpoint" **Kip M.**

► Let's get this straight. The supporters of the War are Burkeians and Neo-Hayekians? Hmm. You centrally plan the absolute change of another State without any tacit knowledge—or even much overt knowledge—of the culture. You do it because you have a theory of politics you want to prove.

Wow. I understand, though. Take Hayek's *Use of Knowledge in Society*, or Burke's speeches on the East India Bill, his *Reflections on the French Revolution*, or the speeches on Warren Hastings Impeachment. Sure, on the surface they seem to indicate that the Iraq war is the exact kind of thing radical ideologues, without any appreciation of the idea of self-organization, would inflict, with maximal pain, on a historically evolved order. But that is just the surface, man! See, you go out and you buy Leo Strauss's[21] special lemon juice, and you rub that juice on the pages. And hey Presto! It turns out that Hayek and Burke, oh so prophetically, say the same things: FOLLOW PRESIDENT BUSH LIKE ROBOTS.

Those conservative intellectuals. They get more impressive by the month. **roger**

► There is definitely a breed of intellectually curious, impatient young men who, due to not being well read in any real sense but already feeling themselves superior to others, latch onto conservative "philosophy" or whatever you want to call it—as a weapon to use against others.

I know that I was seduced by the right-wing propaganda machine for a while in high school, just because I was in the mood to be opposed to the "liberal" stuff we were learning in high school (ironically enough, I now think I had a great high school education, all things considered, and regret feeling like I was superior to the ideas I was learning). As soon as I went away to college and there wasn't as much pressure to try to start conversations with my dad based on Rush Limbaugh, I pretty much stopped caring about whether progressive taxation was like the Holocaust, then when Bush became the Republican nominee, I realized what a farce the whole thing was.

(I come from a religious tradition that encourages personal testimonies, and Republicanism.) **Adam K.**

► There's an anti-theoretical strain in conservative thinking going back to Burke's animadversions on "theorists" in the *Reflections*. But here is the liberal/left critique—as soon as one announces this opposition to theory—to a tendency to derive political policy from an ideology, rather than the natural order, seen as that order that emerges in a culture over time and circumstances—one is, however discretely, announcing a theory. I find Burke's reaction to the French Revolution exemplary in this regard—partly because Burke was so sensitive to the antithesis himself. It is hard to read the letters on the Regicidal Peace without hearing the strains of an ideology. In other words, to fight for an order, rather than to fight within an order, requires some reflection on the order.

Hazlitt, I think, was the first to see this—although Wollenscraft also apparently did. No matter how hard the conservative disposition tries to substitute a sensibility for dialectic, it keeps getting drawn into its logical contradictions—and its solutions to those contradictions. **roger**

The American Street
Author: Digby
February 25, 2004
www.reachm.com/amstreet/archives/000298.html

The American Street is a group blog with a liberal view. This blog entry is by Digby of Hullabaloo (http://digbysblog.blogspot.com). Although the topic is the "gay marriage" amendment discussed earlier, Digby's larger theme is the nation's partisan struggle.

Welcome To Our Nightmare, Mr. Rove

The Rev. Louis Sheldon, head of the Traditional Values Coalition, told *The New York Times* after Bush's announcement: "Call it same-sex marriage, civil unions or domestic partnership, it is all part of a carefully calculated campaign to provide the appearance of normalcy to homosexual behavior . . . It will be unmasked and defeated and President Bush's leadership on this issue will make the difference."

Nick Confessore at TAPPED, Josh Marshall, Noam Schrieber and Ryan Lizza at TNR and others have been discussing at great length the politics of the Banning of Gay Marriage Amendment and have pinpointed, I believe, the essential dilemma Bush faces, and it's good news for us.

First of all, the polls suggest that this will not be the wedge issue that various anonymous administration officials are telling the press it is. That is just fodder for the religious right dupes. The truth is that the genie is way, way out of the bottle on gay rights, and even those with a brain the size of a peanut can see that.

For instance:

"Will and Grace," a formulaic, middle of the road, entirely predictable sit-com that happens to feature two gay male characters in leading and recurring roles, is regularly a top-ten rated program. This is significant mainly because the median age of viewers is 46.2 years of age and garners the second highest national advertising rates on prime time at $414,500 a 30 second spot. Out there in the heartland, fat and happy Muricans are being entertained regularly by a couple of gay cosmopolitans, and the faghags who love them and sponsors are willing to pay top dollar to get their message out to them. (On the other hand, if the three "Queer Eye For the Straight Guy" specials had been counted as a regular series last summer, it would have tied for the #5 rating of the summer in 18–49 age group. Young people aren't threatened by the scourge of gayness, either.)

Why do I bring this up? Because this issue has been decided already. It's over. Most Americans are past the idea that gay people are a threat and this is born out by the free market of popular entertainment. The networks don't show this stuff if it doesn't make money and network shows don't make money if they don't hit a certain broadbased critical mass. People would not be inviting gay people into their homes if they weren't comfortable with them. More than that, they wouldn't watch in great numbers if they didn't like them.

This gay marriage issue is actually the final battle in a war that's already been won.

Karl Rove knows this, which is why he didn't want to have Bush endorse a constitutional amendment. But, he had to and we Democrats really should have some sympathy for him because we've been in his shoes many, many times.

As Noam Schreiber points out in his article:[22]

> . . . this development calls into question Karl Rove's
> entire meta-strategy of courting the conservative base
> for three years on the expectation that, by the fourth,

he and Bush would have built up enough capital to move to the center. That's the kind of thing that could work for a Democratic president, who'd have the benefit of dealing with a bunch of interest groups willing to be bought off. But, as we've seen now on immigration reform and gay marriage and spending and the deficit (e.g., the reaction to the aborted Mars mission and last fall's Medicare reform bill), conservative politics don't work that way . . . it doesn't do them any good to win on 99 issues and lose on the hundredth. If you really think the outcome of that hundredth issue determines whether or not the country is going to hell, then you don't take a whole lot of comfort from having won on the previous 99.

His thesis, basically, is that Republicans are temperamentally unable to compromise because they see things in black and white Manichean terms—otherwise known as Yer-With-Us-Or-Agin-Us, My-Way-Or-The-Highway or the I'll-Hold-My-Breath-Until-I-Turn-Blue philosophy of politics. He further explains that Democrats' collection of interest groups means that activists who agitate for certain issues like gay rights or choice are more willing to compromise because they are usually personally affected by government and are therefore more apt to feel the immediate consequences of incremental change. (Regardless of the motivation, it seems to me that Democrats are just more "into nuance," e.g., smarter.)

What he does not point out, however, is that if this description of the Republicans' political viewpoint is correct it illustrates why they are fundamentally unqualified to govern in a democratic system. If one is unwilling to compromise, then any kind of bipartisan consensus is impossible and rule by force becomes inevitable.

This is undoubtedly why we have seen a steady encroachment of the constitution in the last few years. First came the impeachment, the nuclear option of partisan warfare. Then we saw the Supreme Court intervene in a presidential election despite a clear constitutional roadmap for dealing with just such a situation. Now they are preemptively endorsing the radical idea of a constitutional amendment to remedy a supposed problem that has not even been decided by more than two state supreme courts and one act of civil disobedience in California. (And, if California is any guide, amending the constitution will shortly become the default strategy for all of the right wing's pet causes.)

Karl Rove, however, has to win this election in a system that requires that his boy at least feint to the middle. His strategy, as Schreiber delineates above, didn't work. There is no pleasing the right wing and there is no room for compromise. And, he is learning, just as the centrist Dems learned in the 90s when they tried to maintain a bipartisan consensus, that if you give these wing-nuts an inch, they'll take a mile. The more you move to the right, the more they move to the right. There is no meeting half way.

Welcome to our nightmare, Mr Rove.

The good news is that this kind of politics always leads to the Republicans' inevitable downfall: hubris. The hideous mug of Newt Gingrich became the symbol of GOP hubris when he shut down the government in 1995 and ensured Bill Clinton's re-election the next year. Gingrich finally lost his job when they once again pushed too hard, impeached Clinton over a sexual indiscretion and the public repudiated them at the polls. That is the main reason why Junior hid all the congressional hacks at the RNC convention and ran as a "compassionate conservative," after all. They'd been burned by their right wing.

The banning of gay marriage amendment will, I predict, end up the same way. Americans may not be "in favor" of gay marriage (the idea is quite recent to most people, after all), but neither are they intolerant of gay people or against gay rights. That bridge has been crossed and without mainstream homophobia the anti-gay marriage argument falls apart. "Will and Grace" being a top-ten rated network show proves that mainstream America is perfectly comfortable with gay people in their lives.

Just as a majority of Americans pragmatically understood that married men are sometimes unfaithful, but that's not a reason to shred the constitution, so too will they recognize that there is no good reason that a bunch of religious zealots and take-no-prisoners Republican fanatics should be allowed to use the constitution to discriminate against its own citizens.

The Mahablog
Author: Barbara O'Brien
November 19, 2003
www.mahablog.com/2003.11.16_arch.html#1069255131706

It's my book. It's my blog. And I can snark if I want to.

Do As We Say. . .
Conservatives react to hatred of Bush with shock and alarm and chiding. Hate is *bad*, you know.

Douglas MacKinnon writes in today's *Atlanta Journal-Constitution*:

> "Hate" is a strong, obscene and destructive word, and yet it is being uttered with more frequency by many on the left and by many who should know better. The crass and childish name-calling directed at Bush by candidates for the Democratic presidential nomination not only creates more hate and anger but should bring shame to those in that party who would choose statesmanship and honor over insults and partisanship.
> —Douglas MacKinnon,
> "Hate Is Everywhere and Gets Us Nowhere,"
> *The Atlanta Journal-Constitution*, November 19, 2003

MacKinnon goes on to say (you'll love this), "To be fair, hate was the fuel that energized many on the right during their diatribes against former President Clinton."

Oh, yes, we have to be *fair*, don't we? After more than a decade of unrelenting, visceral, viscious, destructive hate coming at the Left from the Right, the Democratic Party base finally has roused itself and demanded that its leaders stop being appeasers and *fight back*, dammit. And the Right is shocked to see the face of hate, proving they rarely look into mirrors. (Or maybe they look but don't cast a reflection. That was a joke.)

Most conservative commentators are able, grudgingly, to admit that partisan hatred flows both ways. However, they rationalize that liberal hate is more evil than conservative hate.

> Liberals hate conservatives and vice versa, but there's a difference in the way they view each other. Conserva-

tives believe liberalism is a wrongheaded system of government. Many liberals, however, don't accept conservatism as a system of government at all. For them, conservatives are simply ignorant, or, alternately, greedy and self-serving people who refuse to countenance measures for the common good because they put their own interests above the common good.

—Jay Bryant,
"Neanderthals, Angevins and Kennedys,"
Townhall.com, November 19, 2003

(Call me a nit-picker, but I don't consider either "conservatism" or "liberalism" to be *systems* of government. A *system* of government might be a constitutional monarchy or representative democracy or totalitarian communism. "Conservatism" and "liberalism" are political philosophies or sets of values that help form one's worldview and opinions. Further, these philosophies shift from time to time and context to context. For example, a "conservative" in a monarchy supports the power and authority of the monarch, whereas a "conservative" in the U.S. claims to be in favor of limited government.)

Mr. Bryant goes on to blame the schools of America for liberalism, since schools teach more Marx than von Mises, never mind that American liberals are not Marxists. (And never mind that, unlike von Mises, Marx had an enormous impact on world history. To be "fair," they should get equal time.) Bryant says that since schools teach students to be liberals, liberals are therefore people who just accept what they are taught without thinking about it too much.

And Mr. Bryant has oh, so carefully thought out the distinction between a system of government and a political philosophy, not to mention the gaping chasm between Marxism and American liberalism. Right.

A conservative commentator named Bruce Walker complained in today's *American Daily* that he gets hate mail from "Leftists." The email he receives from conservatives is "brief, honest and civil," he says. Leftists, on the other hand, do nothing but "insult, snicker and defame." With a keen grasp of political science (not), he continues,

Picture those who question the Leftist monopoly on truth and morality just as a good Leftist working for

Himmler would picture a stereotypical Jew before the Nazis savagely murdered the Jew. Anyone who holds a conservative position—after you and your friends have gone to the trouble of lecturing and hectoring him for years and years—must simply be ignorant, dumb, bigoted or evil.

The Leftist ad hominem attack need not be bounded by logic. Hitler and his fellow Leftists had no problem simultaneously describing Jews as stupid and clever, as inferior and powerful. What is good enough for the Leftist leaders of Nazi Germany is good enough for modern Leftists.

—Bruce Walker, "Love Letters from Leftists,"
American Daily, November 19, 2003

(The "Hitler was a Leftist" meme has been spreading for several years, and I've learned from experience you can't argue those infected out of it, so there's no point in trying. But for the record: Political science puts Hitler and his fascist totalitarians on the Right, not the Left.)

Dear reader, I can see you quivering in righteous indignation, preparing to insult, snicker at, and defame Mr. Walker. I understand exactly how you feel. However, let me suggest that you apply that pent-up energy toward something worthwhile, like grouting the bathroom tile or volunteering for the Dem candidate of your choice. Trust karma that Mr. Walker will receive all the insults, snickers, and defamation he deserves. But if you do email him, be sure to include a link to the Democratic Underground Hate Mailbag archive.[23]

After Timothy McVeigh killed 168 people in Oklahoma City on April 19, 1995, President Clinton and others asked that the right-wing hate speech that had infested and inspired McVeigh be toned down. Not only did the right-wing hatemongers refuse to take responsibility; they held up Clinton's words as a call to arms to become even more hateful.[24] In fact, one sect of Right-wing haters goes so far as to blame Oklahoma City on Iraq.[25]

There are good reasons—spiritual, moral, and political—to avoid indulging in hate. Hating back the haters just causes hate to escalate.

But neither can haters be reasoned out of their hatred (especially when they are so delusional they cannot recognize their own hatred as hatred), nor can they be appeased through compromise. So how does one deal with them, assuming they can be dealt with?

And is there an objective measure that distinguishes "hate speech" from legitimate criticism? For example, if I say that Tom DeLay is seriously twisted, is that hate speech or a clinical observation?

Whatever. We liberals seem to have reached an impasse. Hate them back, and we lose. Try to reason with them to appease them, and we lose. However, the spiral of hate cannot continue indefinitely—in time, the Tao brings all things into balance. Let's just be sure we keep our heads, so that when the flush comes, we don't go down with it.

Comments

► "We liberals seem to have reached an impasse. Hate them back, and we lose. Try to reason with them to appease them, and we lose."

I recall some freshman college course, where a professor ripped some scales off my mind by pointing out the Western, or perhaps American, tendency to think there were only two sides to any story, only two ways to look at anything, only two solutions to any problem. Hint, hint.

We needn't hate nor try futile reasoning. Satire is good. Words of love and solicitude are good, and what's more, usually infuriating to the right-wing dirty mouths.

You are right about hating back. Bad karma. F***s up everyone, the system, and the possibility for understanding.

I don't know what MacKinnon means about the "childish name-calling directed at Bush by candidates for the Democratic presidential nomination" . . . I have not heard anything but fair descriptions of Bush's presidency, such as incompetent, self-destructive, and likely to increase hatred for Americans all over the world.

As Bush continues to fumble along, year after year, I have come to detest him less and feel sorry for him more. I am convinced the poor guy doesn't have a clue. He does not understand the world, his vision is limited, his imagination is stuck in Hollywood, and he is in thrall to the Vice President. He needs a break. Those people who really love him, right, middle or left, for whatever reason, can do Bush no better favor than to vote in 2004 to retire him to Crawford. **Doran**

► I have several posts on this subject on my blog [Cup o' Joe; http://cupojoe.blogspot.com]: most notably how Republicans are expert at *Framing The Message*.[26] Since these articles are all coming out now, it seems to me that this was part of one of those weekly right-wing meetings at the Heritage Foundation: *OK let's start ratcheting up the noise: paint liberals as hateful!*

As Molly Ivins wrote in her powerful article, "Hatred of Bush? Not Here":[27]

> I would like to remind all the lock-step conservatives that there is a difference between hatred and anger. What you are looking at in this country is not hatred of Bush—a perfectly affable guy—but a growing anger.

I make no bones about being angry, and I have no qualms about using that anger against Republicans and the right-wing b*****ds that have taken over this country. I don't want George Bush dead, like so many on the right wanted Clinton dead. Personally, I hope they all lead happy, prosperous lives. But as long as they continue to screw with me and make my life harder, I will use every legal means at my disposal to fight them.

Be magnanimous in victory, but be victorious first, that's my motto. **Joe V.**

► Being a pacifist who does not condone anyone's hate, I must agree with you and Ivins about the difference between hate and justified anger. I feel anger toward Bush, but I don't hate him at all. I do hate his policies and his party's political platform. I do believe he is a terrorist, et al., but that is due to his murderous actions. But if any emotion wells in me toward the man, it would have to anger. And yes, I feel sorry for him, as well as for all those, whatever their guiding philosophy, who hate other people. **Natalie D.**[28]

► Another favorite right-wing strategy is the "bored by liberals strategy" or the one where they feign inquisitiveness, i.e.: "What is it about George Bush that upsets so many liberals?" They then usually answer that liberals are vehemently against something like "bravery," "steadfastness," "defending the country" or something. No one who ever asks this rhetorical question ever comes up with the sane answer: Liberals hate Bush because he opposes every liberal program, philosophy and idea that we hold dear. It's pretty obvious. It's like asking, "What was it about Strom Thurmond that upset so many blacks?" and coming up with the answer that blacks must not like old people. Insane. **Scout**

► Words like *hate, anger* all stem from fear. I have never been so afraid for my future, my country and my family and their families. We are afraid; we turn to anger and hate to cover up, thus not facing the fear we all feel. I remember what Jesse Jackson said during the 2000 campaign (I am not an admirer of J. Jackson) "do not go into the bushes, you do not want to go into the bushes." Well, we found out. I read this column and have donated $200 to Howard Dean. I challenge everyone who reads this to donate to the candidate of their choice. This is the only way we can get out of the bushes. **Mary**

Wizbang
Author: Paul

May 12, 2004
http://wizbangblog.com/archives/002455.php

A Partisan Beheading?

I found the blogosphere's response to the Nick Berg story interesting.

Kevin[29] put the link up to the video and I put it on one of my extra servers. That started a flood of activity. As you can see below we got 17 trackbacks (and counting)[30] and an Instalanche[31] for good measure.

But I noticed something about the links. . . With the notable exception of Oliver Willis not a single major left-wing blog linked it. The answer was obvious, of course, the lefties hate Kevin because he scares them so they would be linking to the video on a left wing site . . . Right? Right?

So I took a stroll.

Ted,[32] over at Crooked Timber, was still beating the Abu Ghraib drum but acknowledged as an afterthought that he thought the beheading was bad.

Kevin Drum[33] did call it barbaric but then went on to lament that it might make us dedicated to winning the war on terror and of course found time to blame us for Abu Ghraib.

Matthew Yglesias[34] was imitating the third monkey. If there was any evil in it, he wasn't going to speak about it. You would think he would have been moved enough to at least mention it.

Josh Marshall[35] thought he would make a better third monkey than Matt.

Atrios[36] just could not bring himself to mention how Nick Berg was slaughtered but blamed the whole thing on George Bush.

Kos[37] had a post titled "Why Berg was Murdered" and his answer was "The neocons WANTED it this way."

Not a single lefty site linked to the video. I was struck by one thing surfing lefty sites. The anger and animosity for the beheading was not aimed at the guy with the knife but at George Bush.

So I went and looked at right-wing sites . . .

(BTW The Ecosystem was down so I might have missed some big names on either side as I did this from memory.)

Andrew Sullivan[38] took turns first bashing Al Qaeda and then the media and then Al Qeada again. His outrage quotient was pretty high. Called Al Qaeda "dumb" and trashed the media for not putting out the link to the original site.

LGF [Little Green Footballs] OK I did not go . . . They were all over it, trust me. (There were multiple links to the video earlier in the day in the comments.)

Stephen Green[39] wanted to know, "Where's the outrage over this story?" and in a later post said it should get the same media as the prison abuse story.

James Joyner[40] was uncharacteristically late on this story but characteristically compendious. (Update: James linked it when it woke up.)

Michele[41] gave us a reminder who the enemy was and what kind of ~~people~~ animals they were.

Glenn Reynolds[42] has his say and links to the video.

Wizbang! Well, CHECK! And a recursive check at that!

~~A clear majority~~ All but one of the right-wing blogs linked to the video (or said the media should have).

So there you have it . . . a partisan beheading. If the lefties even mentioned it, they downplayed it and could only muster a sense of outrage at George Bush. The folks on the right were far more outraged and actually pointed their outrage at the murderers.

Interesting.

The American Street
Author: Jay Bullock
May 12, 2004
www.reachm.com/amstreet/archives/000765.html#more

"Violence Doesn't End Violence"

So says Mariane Pearl, mother of Adam Pearl and husband of the late Daniel Pearl. You probably remember Danny Pearl; he was 2002's Nick Berg. (2003's Nick Berg was supposed to be Jessica Lynch, but she is not following the script.)

Last night here in Milwaukee, Mariane Pearl spoke as a part of a local lecture series known as "From the Heart." Other speakers on the list are Fergie, Naomi Judd, and Sharon Stone. Also included in the series, though, was Kim Phuc Phan Thi, who most of you probably recognize from this picture.[43] (Here's what she looks like now.[44]) Caveat: I did not actually see either lecture, Pearl's or Phan Thi's.

I'm not really known for writing about the war. I started blogging for real only about a year ago, a while after "Mission Accomplished," and in the run-up to the war I let others more qualified than I make the case against it. But, by accident of geography, I have something to say about it now, from Mariane Pearl and Kim Phuc Phan Thi, who recently graced my town with their presence.

We can blame the death of Nick Berg on anyone we want, it seems. Al Qaeda is an easy one, though the terrorist in question, Abu Musab al-Zarqawi, was at best only a sometime ally of Osama bin Laden, not full-blown al Qaeda. CBS is another easy target, one that conservatives have not neglected, for airing photos of Abu Ghraib torture. We can blame the Abu Ghraib culprits. Or the Iraqi police and US forces that held Berg past his scheduled departure date. Or Rumsfeld. Or the Bush administration in general (especially with news that given the chance to capture Zarqawi, the administration passed to bolster its case for war).

But I like what Mariane Pearl said about the matter:

Those who killed Danny and those who killed Nicholas
Berg are despicable people but violence doesn't end
violence . . . It's a horrendous murder similar to the one
Danny went through, and proof that violence leads to
violence. This cycle of violence is not likely to end.
—Meg Jones, "Pearl Mourns for Berg's Family,"
The Milwaukee Journal Sentinel, May 11, 2004

Terrorists like al-Zarqawi (or al Qaeda) don't need an Abu Ghraib
to retaliate for, of course. They are fighting what they perceive to be a
war against decades, if not centuries, of Western aggression and oppression, of which Bush's War is just the latest example. Anyone with even a
passing familiarity with the Israeli-Palestinian conflict knows that eye-
for-an-eye revenge cycles solve nothing and advance no causes but
bloody violence.

Kim Phuc Phan Thi speaks out against these cycles of violence
whenever she can. She's a UNESCO Goodwill Ambassador for Peace,
and sees her role as a peace activist as divine. "God used me that day,"
she says about the day her village was napalmed and the infamous
photograph was taken. By most accounts, the image of a naked,
burned, screaming child on the cover of every major daily paper in this
country began the turning of the tide. Public support for the Vietnam
war ebbed, and serious questions about our tactics and conduct in the
war followed. Phan Thi, since her defection to Canada in 1992, has
continued the work for peace that her picture began. "Sometimes I like
to think of that little girl, screaming, running up the road, as being not
just a symbol of war, but a symbol of a cry for peace," she says in her
speeches.

The photos (and, potentially, video) from Abu Ghraib, before they
were replaced in our consciousness by images of Nick Berg, could have
been the same turning point in this war as Phan Thi's was in Vietnam.
They may yet be. And what disturbs me most about them, aside from
the very real chance that the tactics depicted therein were not just
sanctioned but ordered by U.S. commanders, is the underlying current
of payback. This includes new allegations that some of the abusers/
torturers very clearly had Jessica Lynch in mind as they performed their
outrages at Abu Ghraib and in particular Camp Bucca.

I said before that Jessica Lynch is not following the script that Danny Pearl and Nick Berg did, and by that, I don't mean that she escaped death. I mean that Pearl's death did fuel and Berg's death is currently fueling very real, very dangerous levels of "Let's go kill us some brown-skinned people!" Don't believe me? Drop by some bastions of the right blogosphere, like LGF, the Freepers, or those rottweiler guys.

But Lynch, like Phan Thi and Mariane Pearl, is not calling for more blood. She is not calling for genocide, extermination, carpet bombing. She is not enabling the bloodthirsty mob.

And the Berg family, too, is placing the blame somewhere besides the Muslim world. They are laying the blame squarely on us. To an extent, this is because Nick Berg was detained by Iraqi police and (possibly) CPA [Coalition Provisional Authority] forces. But the Bergs were against this war from the start. They knew, as I did, and probably many of you, that taking revenge on Saddam Hussein and the Iraqi people—for surely innocents would die—was not the answer to any reasonable question. It was not a key step in the "war on terror" or toward advancing any plausible national interest. It was Bush's revenge for the Gulf War's failures; it was the American public's revenge for 9/11 after bin Laden proved illusive and Afghanistan proved unsatisfactory.

Listen to those who know, please. Listen to Jessica Lynch, Mariane Pearl, Kim Phuc Phan Thi: Violence does not end violence!

Endnotes

[1] For another perspective, see David Neiwert, "Jingoes and the Fascist Impulse," Orcinus, May 22, 2004 (http://dneiwert.blogspot.com/2004_05_16_dneiwert_archive.html#108529693168032263).

[2] www.crookedtimber.org/archives/001810.html.

[3] Jonah Goldberg is a nationally syndicated columnist and the editor of *National Review Online*. You may read the referenced column at www.nationalreview.com/thecorner/04_03_28_corner-archive.asp#028261

[4] The Decembrist, http://markschmitt.typepad.com/decembrist.

[5] TAP, *The American Prospect* magazine. You may read the column referenced at www.prospect.org/web/page.ww?section=root&name=ViewWeb&articleId=7765.

[6] Matthew Yglesias responds to Goldberg at www.matthewyglesias.com/archives/week_2004_05_16.html#003400.

[7] Kevin Drum responds to Goldberg at www.washingtonmonthly.com/archives/individual/2004_03/003574.php.

[8] Goldberg discusses his mail at www.nationalreview.com/thecorner/04_05_16_corner-archive.asp#032296.

[9] Jacob Levy writes for The Volokh Conspiracy, a very popular group blog. Levy responds to Goldberg at http://volokh.com/archives/archive_2004_05_21.shtml#1085178873.

[10] www.law.cornell.edu/topics/critical_theory.html.

[11] Yglesias, *ibid.*

[12] Henry Farrell blogs at Crooked Timber. You may read the blog post referenced at www.crookedtimber.org/archives/001360.html.

[13] http://examinedlife.typepad.com/johnbelle/2003/11/dead_right.html.

[14] http://examinedlife.typepad.com/johnbelle/2003/12/dead_right_agai.html.

[15] http://examinedlife.typepad.com/johnbelle/2003/09/conservatism_co.html.

[16] http://examinedlife.typepad.com/johnbelle/2003/09/conservatism_co_1.html.

[17] You may read Goldberg's reply to Balko at www.nationalreview.com/thecorner/03_05_04_corner-archive.asp#008358.

[18] Radley Balko blogs at the Agitator (www.theagitator.com).

[19] You may read Goldberg's thoughts on consistency at www.nationalreview.com/thecorner/03_05_04_corner-archive.asp#008365.

[20] David Frum, *Dead Right* (Basic Books, 1995).

[21] Leo Strauss (1899-1973) was a German political philosopher whose ideas are currently in vogue in some conservative circles. Strauss believed that a nation should be led by an elite few, and these elites are obligated to practice deception on the masses to maintain power and national unity.

[22] www.tnr.com/etc.mhtml.

[23] www.democraticunderground.com/mail/index.html.

[24] www.stopmediaregulation.org/theplayers/clinton.htm.

[25] www.newsmax.com/commentarchive.shtml?a=2002/4/28/211241.

[26] Joe V. blogs about framing the message at http://cupojoe.blogspot.com/106730977185327901.

[27] Molly Ivins, "Hatred of Bush? Not Here" (Creators Syndicate/ *The Ft. Worth Star Telegram*, October 19, 2003).

[28] Natalie D. blogs at All Facts and Opinions (http://gratefuldread.net).

[29] Kevin Aylward is principal blogger at Wizbang.

[30] The trackbacks are not published here.

[31] A spike in web traffic brought on by a link on Instapundit.

[32] Ted Barlow blogs about the Abu Ghraib prison scandal at www.crookedtimber.org/archives/001839.html. Also in the comments section of the Wizbang blog post, not reproduced here, Barlow writes, "God forbid that I should 'bang the drum' about Abu Gharib, but the original post that you're pointing to was put up before I read about the beheading. Not to mess up your theory or anything."

[33] You may read Kevin Drum's comments at www.washingtonmonthly.com/archives/individual/2004_05/003893.php.

[34] No specific Yglesias post was linked. Yglesias discussed the Berg beheading after this Wizbang post was published, for example, www.matthewyglesias.com/archives/week_2004_05_16.html#003349.

[35] No specific Marshall comment was linked. Marshall discussed the Berg beheading after this Wizbang post was published, for example, www.talkingpointsmemo.com/archives/week_2004_05_16.php#002969.

[36] You may read Atrios's comments at http://atrios.blogspot.com/2004_05_09_atrios_archive.html#108430197190583603.

[37] You may read the comments on Daily Kos at www.dailykos.com/story/2004/5/12/01637/8395. There were earlier comments on the murder of Berg at www.dailykos.com/story/2004/5/11/14526/6522. The video was linked in the Daily Kos diary section, but not on the main page.

[38] Wizbang does not link to a specific AndrewSullivan blog, but may have been referring to this one: www.andrewsullivan.com/index.php?dish_inc=archives/2004_05_09_dish_archive.html#108430254061929023.

[39] Wizbang did not link to a specific VodkaPundit blog post, and I could not find the quotation. Stephen Green posted a blog called "Where's the Outrage?" on May 12, however: www.vodkapundit.com/archives/005841.php.

[40] You may read Joyner's comments at www.outsidethebeltway.com/archives/006100.html.

[41] A Small Victory, http://asmallvictory.net/archives/006807.html.

[42] www.instapundit.com/archives/015500.php.

[43] www.gallerym.com/pixs/photogs/pulitzer/pages/vietnam_napalm.htm. The photo—perhaps the most famous image of the Vietnam war—shows a group of Vietnamese children, one of them an unclothed young girl (Phan Thi), running down a road to escape a nepalm attack, followed by a group of US soldiers.

[44] www.onwisconsin.com/fromtheheart/slideshow3.asp.

A P P E N D I X

The Clark Sphere

*This post from September 13, 2003 (http://theclarksphere.com/archives/
000249.html) was written by Stirling Newberry, who blogs on The
Blogging of the President and elsewhere. He was instrumental in the Draft
Wesley Clark movement in the fall of 2003. Although written with the
Draft Clark movement in mind, Newberry's comments speak to the way
mass media has changed, and damaged, America's political landscape.*

The Sphere Versus the Pyramid

The Nature of Top Down Politics

I don't tell faerie stories much, and "once upon a time, long ago in
1960, when television changed the presidential race" is a story too often
told. But the basic point is there—television, and other modern media
based on high enough quality reproduction—records, television, color
cinema—changed society. It was the information form of the top down
society. Mass production meant top down design, and it gradually
found a top down way of communicating. One can trace the growth of
top down, in manufacturing, in media, in thinking in general.

The power of the pyramid was overwhelming—it changed society
in a thousand ways. We remember some of the positive ones, because a
top down media pointed at any image—from segregated water foun-
tains, to young men in Vietnam, to a political figure—could propel
action on that image. For a time, the top down media changed every-

thing, and created an ecstatic philosophy of media freedom that was espoused by philosopher Marshal MacLuhan. It seemed that anyone could be empowered by the channel just by getting its attention.

The Clark movement is based on a new form of organization, one that is taking root through micromedia, the Internet, and the relationships they make possible—the expanding sphere.

If you ask many of the people who are in the Draft movement how they first saw Wesley Clark, they will answer "CNN." Now, CNN does not reach a large audience on the cosmic scale of things, but it has a devoted following, especially when there are fast moving, unfolding, and complex stories. Stories with a compelling message. If you ask them how they found out about there being a movement to draft Clark, they will say John Hlinko and Draft Wesley Clark.[1]

John didn't get major media broadcast campaigns—his first big strike was a simple on-air commercial that ran in a limited area. On radio. But it was so unusual, it was picked up on Meet the Press, and events carried things from there.

If that were the story—hit and run—then John Edwards, Gephardt, even Dennis Kucinich or Mosley-Braun—could be here. But they aren't. And that is because the story didn't end with a small commercial that became a gateway—it is what people found on the other side of that gateway. They found, and will find, a growing and complex community of ideas, and a social organization that drives the message forward and upward. It is a more powerful force than personal bonds—even people who do not know each other, or talk to each other, are woven together by it.

But what is it? And why did it work here, and in so many other places?

►►►

The sphere is not merely "grass roots." *Grass roots* is a phrase, if you think about it, that is a product of the world being top down dominated. In order to push back, the flattened bottom of society had to develop social organization that dealt with the pervasive reality of the media. To get the message out, one had to be numerous—with a short slogan, or one had to be offbeat and hope to be a cult phenomenon—or one had to attack some micro problem relentlessly for years.

An example of the first is, of course, a peace movement. "No War" is about as short a slogan as it gets. There are numerous examples of the second, protest candidates of all kinds come to mind. The third dominated the intellectual sphere of politics for years—a single, small, change, which it could be argued had no effect on anything else. A health regulation for example, removing one dam, freeing one person. Micro issues with small core of super committed people.

The book that documents the rise of top down media is from the historian of American social organization in the post-modern era: David Halberstam, and the book is *The Powers That Be*.[2] The growth of networks, and their gradual conversion into power pyramids is the story of what is now called "the old media."

The power of media was that it could electrify the nation like a shock. For a nation which built its political and economic system on mobilizing people, the top down media seemed like the answer—it could, for a short time, focus the entire attention of the nation on one problem, one social ill, and give it a face that could be remembered.

This media gradually forced a few specific forms of campaigning, it also forced the drive for absolute and total control over every aspect of message—one loose image, and the ship of state sinks. Nixon's not shaving is the story that was told, but I remember the day the infamous tank picture came out in the Dukakis campaign, someone remarked "Great, we are working for snoopy the wonder beagle." From the Next President of The United States, to a joke, in moments.

Many books were written about how the left could start to "win" in this environment; however, what none of them realized was a simple fact—the entire paradigm was either to be at the top of the pyramid, which favors obsessive control, or at the bottom, in which case one is either reactive, or ideologically rigid. None of these models—whether it was the Clintonian triangulation, the DLC run in fear from any image which might allow the Republicans to attack, or the Green model of an ideologically driven party of the left—worked for long as a governing model. Clinton could administer brilliantly, perhaps the best use of executive power, as purely an executive, of any President who served in the second half of the 20th Century. But he could not win congress, and therefore could not govern.

The left, faced with being either top down or bottom up, fought long theoretical battles, not realizing that the answer was growing right in front of them: the complex and expanding sphere.

►►►

The entry point of the pyramid model is "branded anarchy"; the people at the top don't care what the people at the bottom do, so long as the people at the bottom are walking advertisements for the top, and get other people to support that top—with money or votes. Ultimately, in the branded anarchy universe, everyone is a billboard for whichever pyramid they are part of.

The top down structure then tries to take this and turn the corner to control, or extraction of money—to either expand the power of the pyramid, or create revenues. The pyramid then is powerful, at first, because it offers freedom—if people join with it, they are suddenly part of a vastly more numerous group of people, with the power that moving in sync provides. However, this phase, as the Internet bubble documents, is not profitable. The pyramid cannot easily draw revenue from it, nor can it force those inside of it to do very much. It must go to the next step—which is to lock individuals into it, and make it impossible to switch to some other pyramid—whether network, operating system, political party, church or cell phone company.

The users of a pyramid then want branded anarchy—maximum freedom for them—but they also want smooth experience. And this is how the pyramid ropes them in—it offers to get rid of the hassles of branded anarchy—if they will give up their chance to move to another pyramid. Whether it is the frequent flier program, or the word processor that one can't export the macros from—smoothness for control is the top down universe's game.

Pyramids often clash with other pyramids—and during these short clashes, being able to shift loyalties often rewards consumers quite handsomely. But such clashes generally end. It is more profitable for a pyramid to hold on to its existing customers or followers than to fight. The fights then become peripheral, and well-defined fights for market share among certain consumers who are known to be fickle and irregular anyway.

►►►

Top down politics then became a progressively narrower field, and progressively more focused on the bumper sticker and or the grind of lobbying over a small piece of legislation. One can see why this environment, in the long run, favors the rich lobbyist, the slogan and reactionary politics. It creates people who are reactive, and who view the system as something to be gamed—to give as little as possible, or to play off competitors. The entire nature of pyramids squashed the ability of coherent alternatives—everyone was given an either or choice of pyramids, and could get, at most, one or two price concessions out of them. More than that was not possible.

This nature—of squashing what had once been the vibrant source of ideas—meant that one of the most important political alliances in American politics was broken. That alliance, between the idealistic and academic progressives, and the pragmatic and practical progressives, was the basis for the wave of governmental improvement that began in the 1890s and took final shape with the New Deal. Without this alliance—where ideas were shaped into practical performance driven policy—the idealists were left to criticise and grind away on the tiniest of details, while the pragmatists where left to shift in the middle as "swing" voters between two parties that seemed not to care about them.

The basic nature of micropolitics also encouraged fragmentation. Each interest group had to convince politicians that there was no connection to other demands, no other costs, and no need for a systematic use of political capital. In short, it encouraged making a separate peace on every issue, since, after all, each issue would be driven by those willing to trade everything and anything else for it. Campaigning became promising on microissues, and, as a result, agendas were set before the first day of governing. This fit in with ever-growing gridlock.

It was not a problem with how the game was played, but in the game itself.

To change politics means changing the fundamental model of social organization.

––––––––––

Endnotes

[1] www.draftwesleyclark.com.

[2] David Halberstam, *The Powers That Be* (New York: Alfred A. Knopf, 1979).

The Way of Blogs

———◆———◆———◆———

A good word finds its own market.

—*Tao teh Ching, verse 62*

What About Blogs?

About 1994 I attended a presentation on web-based marketing. I worked for a large publishing company at the time, and some entrepreneurs were eager to set up a company web page. But graphical interface was new, and slow, and clunky, and there wasn't much content on the web at the time. Most of the attendees were unimpressed. I remember telling one fellow, "It'll happen. Give it a couple of years." He was skeptical.

In a couple of years it *was* happening, although to most people purchasing on the web was new and awkward. A great many startups went into and out of business in the next few years as web marketing found its footing. But today e-commerce is a big part of American business. The company I worked for in 1994, since then taken over by another company, is selling books on the web.

Blogs are, in my estimation, about where e-commerce was in 1996. We're just past the clunky phase but still new and mostly unknown. That will change. It must change.

It must change, because what does it say about our country if our political leaders must assemble focus groups and conduct polls to find out what We, the People, think? How can republican government exist when communication flows only one way?

And what do We, the People, think? Those who join in the Great Online Conversation not only are exposed to new ideas; they are also challenged to explain their own ideas. To do that, they have to think, and to clarify their own thoughts. And on the web, anyone's timely, clarified thought, well expressed, truly can be heard around the world.

Blogs will not replace newspapers any more than e-commerce replaced shopping malls. However, in the future I expect blogging to become an established part of our media mix. Newspapers are already establishing blogs on their web sites, as are political parties and other organizations. But I think the individual blogger, the person with something to say and the strong desire to say it, will remain the heart and soul of blogging. Because, unlike mass media, through which governments and corporations and organizations speak, blogging is all about what *one* person has to say.

May all the good words find their place in the market.

Glossary of Blogging Terms

Blogging has developed a unique vocabulary that might be confusing to the uninitiated. This glossary defines terms commonly found on blogs. It assumes the reader has some acquaintance with the Internet.

archive Blog posts that have scrolled off a blog's home page are stored in archives, usually organized by date.

bandwidth The volume of data that can be accessed from a web page within a fixed amount of time. Bandwidth usage is determined by the number of data bytes on a page together with the number of hits on that data. A site receiving an unexpected number of hits may exceed the bandwidth allotted by its host and temporarily shut down.

barking moonbat Extremist; person on the edge of an "ism."

blog 1. noun Short for *web log*, a frequently updated web site in which new items of information appear at the top of the page and older items sink to the bottom. **2. verb** To compose a web log item; to provide information or commentary on a blog. Examples: *Mary blogs about cats. Jim blogged his trip to Spain. I will blog the news conference.*

blogger A person who blogs, especially the owner/proprietor of a blog.

blogosphere The totality of blogs.

blogroll A list of links to blogs, usually a blogger's favorite blogs.

bookmark A web page address (URL) stored by a browser.

browser Software for viewing web pages, such as Internet Explorer or Netscape Navigator.

BTW "By the way."

cluebat Metaphorical implement used for pounding knowledge into someone's head.

dead-tree media Print media; magazines, newspapers.

drinking the Kool-Aid 1. To accept an ideology without thinking. 2. To be fooled by propaganda; particularly, to accept the "official" version of events at face value.

fisking Critical, point-by-point deconstruction of a news story or article in order to refute whatever the article says. A fisked article is usually quoted in detail, with a blogger's commentary inserted into the text. Derived from the name of journalist Robert Fisk, a frequent fisking target on right-wing blogs.

flame To engage in a heated argument.

flame war An online discussion that has degenerated into personal attacks.

group blog A blog with more than one contributing blogger.

hit Delivery of any content on a web site, including but not limited to page views. For example, if a web search delivers an image from a web page but not the whole page, that counts as a hit. See also *page view* and *visit*.

host A computer directly connected to the Internet. For bloggers, a host is a provider of web services. Most bloggers publish their blogs through a commercial hosting service.

HTML Hypertext Markup Language; a system of formatting a document published on a web page. HTML tags are used to create links and determine what a document looks like on the web.

IMO or IMHO ("In My Opinion"; "In My Humble Opinion") Injected in text, indicates the writer admits fallibility.

ISP Internet Service Provider. Most Internet users go through an ISP to access the Internet.

Kool-Aiders People who exhibit obstinate, unshakable devotion to a leader, cause, or ideology.

link Text tagged with the web address of a web page, picture, or other content.

LOL Laughing Out Loud.

meta- The English prefix *meta* (from Greek, meaning "beside" or "after"); when used on the web it usually means "comprehensive" or "about." So, a *metablog* would be a blog about blogs.

meta tag HTML tag with keywords used by search engines.

moonbat See *barking moonbat.*

new media Internet news sources, including blogs.

old media Print, radio, television.

page view To access the HTML-formatted content of a web page. See also *hits* and *visit.*

permalink A link to an individual blog post, enabling a reader to click back to that post even when it has scrolled off the blog's main page into the archives.

ping A "signal" sent from one web site to another. Bloggers send out pings to alert other sites that the blog has been updated.

post 1. verb To publish a blog article or leave a message on a forum. **2. noun** A single message in a forum or blog.

ROTFLMAO Rolling On The Floor, Laughing My A** Off.

RSS (Rich Site Summary or RDF Site Summary) A language application that describes a web site's content available for distribution or syndication to other web users. By using RSS syndication a reader can "subscribe" to a blog so that updates are delivered to a desktop application or by email.

smiley Text arranged to suggest a facial expression, such as the ubiquitous :-).

snark To express derision and ridicule.

snarky irritable.

thread On Internet forums, a *thread* is a message and all of the responses to that message. Visually, a thread often branches or cascades from the original message. Some blogs enable threading of comments.

thread drift A thread conversation that has wandered away from the original topic.

tinfoil hat Metaphorical indicator of mental instability. A person who expresses an outlandish or irrational opinion is said to be wearing a tinfoil hat.

trackback A system that alerts a blogger that another site has linked to a blog post. See also *ping*.

troll **1. verb** To post taunts and insults in a forum or blog, especially one devoted to a belief or cause the troller dislikes. **2. verb** To troll for hits for one's web site by leaving incendiary comments on many forums or blogs. **noun** A person who trolls.

URL "Universal Resource Locator"; a web address.

visit One person's perusal of a web site.

weblog See *blog*.

wiki Programming that allows web users to edit the content of web site, allowing online collaboration.

XML (eXtensible Markup Language) A web data format that allows developers to process data in a standard, consistent way.